STITCH
SAMPLER

· · · · · · · · ◆ · · · · · · ·

STITCH
SAMPLER

• · · · · · · ◆ · · · · · · •

LUCINDA GANDERTON

DK

A DORLING KINDERSLEY BOOK
New York • London • Sydney • Moscow

A DORLING KINDERSLEY BOOK
London, New York, Munich, Melbourne, Delhi

A Penguin Company

**Dedicated to the memory of
Mary Josephine Ganderton,
my mother and my inspiration**

Senior Editor: Mary Lindsay
Senior Art Editor: Sarah Hall
Production Controller: Michelle Thomas
DTP Designer: Jason Little

Managing Editors: Stephanie Jackson, Jonathan Metcalf
Managing Art Editor: Nigel Duffield

Produced by
C&B Packaging Ltd
London House, Great Eastern Wharf
Parkgate Road, London SW11 4NQ

Managing Editor: Kate Yeates
Editor: Heather Dewhurst
US Editor: Barbara Minton
Art Director: Roger Bristow
Art Editor: Helen Collins
Designers: Suzanne Metcalfe-Megginson, Bill Mason
Photography: Sampson Lloyd

First published in Great Britain in 1999
by Dorling Kindersley Limited
80 Strand, London WC2R 0RL

Copyright © 1999 Dorling Kindersley Limited, London
Text copyright © 1999 Lucinda Ganderton
The moral right of Lucinda Ganderton to be identified
as the author of this book has been asserted.

All rights reserved. No part of this publication may be
reproduced, stored in a retrieval system, or transmitted
in any form or by any means, electronic, mechanical,
photocopying, recording or otherwise, without the prior
written permission of the copyright owner.

6 8 10 9 7 5

Library of Congress Cataloging-in-Publication Data
Ganderton, Lucinda
Stitch Sampler / Lucinda Ganderton. – 1st American ed.
p. cm.
Includes index.
ISBN 0-7694-4628-6 (alk. paper)
1. Embroidery. 2. Needlework. I. Title.
TT770.G36 1999
746.44'042–dc21   99–14527
                              CIP

Reproduced by Colourscan Singapore
Printed and bound by Dai Nippon, Hong Kong.
'See our complete catalog at'
www.dk.com

CONTENTS

Introduction

THE ART OF embroidery has been defined simply as the ornamentation of textiles with decorative stitchery. It is an ancient craft which encompasses a wealth of history, and the same stitches are used by embroiderers throughout the world. They provide an international vocabulary that crosses the boundaries of land and time. Local patterns, designs, and ways of working vary from place to place, but the actual stitch techniques do not. The language of stitches is infinitely adaptable. It is being constantly reinterpreted by contemporary stitchers who produce their new work as part of a continuing tradition.

INTERNATIONAL HERITAGE

Sewing was once an essential part of daily life for most women and for some men. Before mass production, many clothes and items of domestic furnishing had to be made at home, and embroidery evolved as a means of decorating and personalising the plain needlework used for household linens and garments.

People in different countries concentrated on their own particular aspects of embroidery and names such as Bokhara couching, Antwerp edging, Portuguese border, and Algerian eye reflect the international aspect of the stitches they used. Creative concepts are always interchanged; patterns and ideas have travelled and developed throughout the world. German immigrants in Pennsylvania, for example, had to adapt their own traditional dense cross-stitch patterns to outline-based designs, because of the shortage of embroidery threads in the New World.

PORTRAIT OF A LADY
Fine silk threads in a subtle range of natural dyes were used to embroider this eighteenth century picture. Layers of straight stitches have been worked in many directions to build up the image.

FLORAL BORDER
Long decorative bands, like this tent stitch pattern in bright Berlin wools, were worked by Victorian ladies and used to adorn cushions and throws.

TYPES OF STITCH

Embroidery stitches are worked on fabric, while needlepoint stitches are sewn onto canvas. Although there are hundreds of individual stitches used for both these techniques, they can be classified into just four groups, according to the way they are constructed: flat stitches which lie on the surface of the fabric; looped stitches, where one stitch is anchored by another; knotted stitches in which the thread is twisted back on itself to form a raised stitch, and openwork stitches which create a regular pattern of spaces, integrating the thread with the background fabric.

USING STITCHES

The various stitches within these four groups are endlessly adaptable and can be used in many ways, depending on the effect required. They can outline a design, be worked closely together so that they conceal the fabric completely, or be spaced further apart to allow the background to show through. Others may be used singly, repeated in rows, or stitched in a solid line.

Certain stitches were developed for particular reasons. Gold thread is costly and too thick to pass easily through the fabric, so couching stitch was used to anchor it to the fabric with small stitches in fine thread. Turkey stitch evolved as an imitation of the cut pile of a rug, and insertion stitches were used as a means of joining two pieces of fabric.

One single stitch may be used throughout a piece of work. Rows of tent and cross stitches are used to create both samplers and embroidered pictures, while straight stitch can be used randomly like a painter's brushstrokes to build up a textured, three-dimensional surface. It is when the patterns and shapes of the various stitches are combined, however, that their full potential is realised.

STITCH NAMES

For many centuries, knowledge of embroidery stitches was handed down as part of the wider folk tradition of needlecraft. It was not until 1631, when *The Needle's Excellency* was printed, that their names began to be formalised in Europe. This was a book of patterns,

COUNTRY GARDEN
This characteristic transfer design from the 1930s features plants worked with French knots, link, fly, and buttonhole stitches, and outlines in stem stitch.

GOLD SLIPPER
Straight stitch flowers in silk floss have been combined with gold thread couched in a swirling pattern to decorate this nineteenth century slipper top, which was never made up.

not a practical manual, and there were no working diagrams or stitch illustrations. Some of the stitches listed – "Fern-stitch," "Chain-stitch," "Back-stitch," and the "Crosse-stitch" – are still in general use. Various other names were adopted over the following centuries. Some described the way in which the actual stitches were made, for example, twisted insertion and back stitch trellis. Others, such as cushion stitch, ladder stitch, window filling, and rope stitch, were named after the objects of daily life that they resembled. Still more were inspired by the surroundings of the natural world: star, wave, cloud, feather, coral, leaf, petal, and wheatear stitches.

Needlework was not valued as a separate area of study until the late nineteenth century. Under the influence of the Arts and Crafts Movement, designers interested in the history of stitching set about examining embroidered fabrics and even unpicked old examples from across the world to discover how they had been worked. New historical texts and instruction books were written, and the format and names of stitches were standardised for the first time.

MIRROR, MIRROR
Shisha stitch highlights the traditional chain stitch design of a contemporary Indian embroidery in silk rayon.

INDIAN PATCHWORK
Fragments of antique fabrics in metallic threads were salvaged and stitched together to make this hanging.

How to Use This Book

The book is divided into six chapters. The first deals with the equipment, threads, and fabrics used for stitchery and the various techniques involved. This is followed by the Gallery of Stitches – a visual library of the 234 stitches featured. The stitch instructions are grouped into four chapters – Lines and Borders, Filling Stitches, Openwork, and Needlepoint – each of which has several sub-sections showing the different types of stitches within the group.

GALLERY OF STITCHES
These pages provide a quick visual reference to all the stitches featured in the book. The name of each one is given, followed by the number of the page where the instructions for working it can be found.

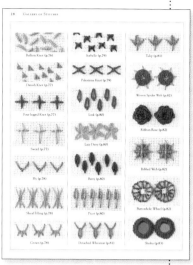

Stitch Instruction Chapters

STITCH EXAMPLE
Illustrates finished appearance of stitch

OTHER NAME
Shows most common alternatives for stitches with two or more names

LEVEL
Indicates the skill level required to make the stitch – easy, intermediate, or advanced

USES
Suggests practical ways in which each stitch can be used or adapted

METHOD
Describes the way in which the stitch is constructed

MATERIALS
Lists type of fabric, thread, and any other equipment needed.

LETTER ANNOTATION
Points at which the needle enters and exits fabric are annotated in alphabetical order

STITCH VARIATION
Shows another stitch which is worked in a similar way to the main stitch.

TECHNIQUE VARIATION
Illustrates a different way of working the stitch or an alternative color scheme.

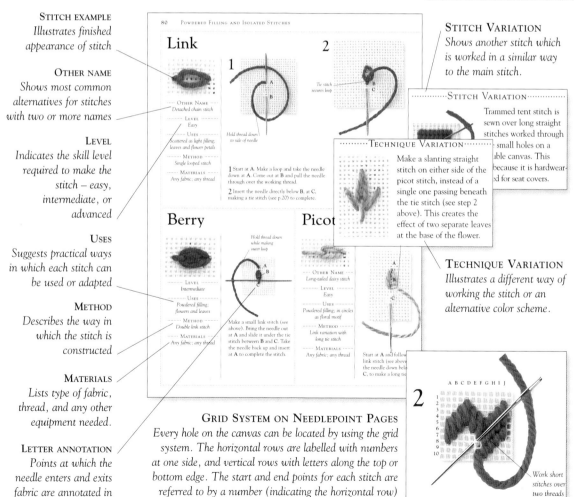

GRID SYSTEM ON NEEDLEPOINT PAGES
Every hole on the canvas can be located by using the grid system. The horizontal rows are labelled with numbers at one side, and vertical rows with letters along the top or bottom edge. The start and end points for each stitch are referred to by a number (indicating the horizontal row) and a letter (indicating the vertical row), eg 9F to 7F.

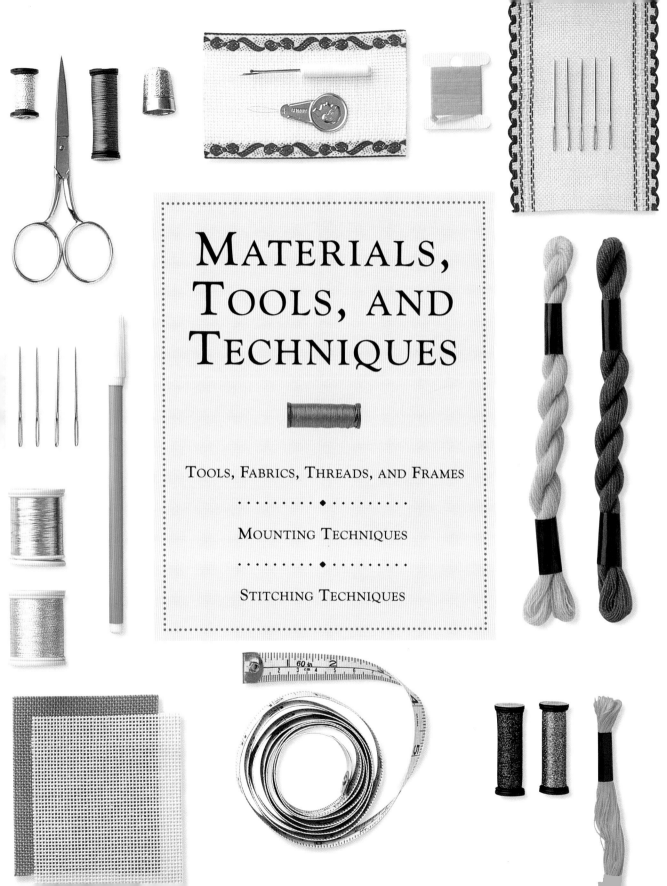

MATERIALS, TOOLS, AND TECHNIQUES

TOOLS, FABRICS, THREADS, AND FRAMES

· · · · · · · · · ◆ · · · · · · · · ·

MOUNTING TECHNIQUES

· · · · · · · · · ◆ · · · · · · · · ·

STITCHING TECHNIQUES

Tools, Fabrics, Threads, and Frames

THE BASIC EQUIPMENT required for embroidery is minimal; as with many other sewing crafts, all that is necessary to start stitching is a needle, a length of thread, a piece of cloth, and a pair of scissors. Much time and care will be invested in creating a finished piece of needlework, so the choice of materials at the outset is important. In order to achieve a professional and long-lasting result it is worth investing in the best quality tools, threads, and fabric, and taking time over their selection.

············ HANDY TIP ············

Sewing boxes designed for embroidery and fabric-lined wicker baskets are the traditional way to keep embroidery equipment together in one place. Art bins and plastic tool boxes from hardware suppliers provide practical alternatives: they are easy to transport and have many compartments in which to store threads, needles, and scissors.

WORKBOX TOOLS

Every workbox should be equipped with two pairs of sharp, steel-bladed scissors: large shears for cutting out cloth or canvas, and pointed embroidery scissors to clip threads and knots. A stitch ripper is convenient for unpicking mistakes and removing tacking. Dressmaker's pencils or pens are used to draw motifs and guidelines directly on to fabric. Choose a pen with fading ink for any items that cannot be washed, or a watersoluble version for those that will be laundered. Chalk pencils leave a fine powdered line which can easily be brushed away. A ruler and tape measure may also prove helpful when marking up designs. A needle threader, pins, and thimble are also useful tools.

THIMBLE

BENT-HANDLED SHEARS

LIQUID MARKING PEN

DRESSMAKER'S PENCIL

TAILOR'S CHALK PENCIL

EMBROIDERY SCISSORS

STITCH RIPPER

NEEDLE THREADER

STRAIGHT PINS

RULER

TAPE MEASURE

FABRIC AND CANVAS

Stitches can be worked on to any fabric, but there is a wide range designed especially for embroidery. Woven from cotton or linen, the square mesh produces regular, even stitches. They are gauged by the count or number of threads to every 1in (2.5cm): the more threads, the finer the fabric. Use soft, single thread evenweave for counted thread, pulled fabric, and drawn thread work; double thread (Aida, Binca, or Hardanger) for geometric patterns and cross stitch; and canvas for needlepoint.

CANVAS
Both single and double weaves come in a variety of weights. Rigid plastic comes in 10-count.

SINGLE CANVAS
(INTERLOCK)

SINGLE CANVAS
(MONO WEAVE)

PLASTIC CANVAS

DOUBLE CANVAS

EVENWEAVE FABRIC
Manufactured in gauges from 8- to 36-count, this is available in many colors and textures.

SINGLE THREAD
EVENWEAVE

BINCA

AIDA CLOTH

PLAINWEAVE FABRIC
Decorative silk, felt, cotton stripes, and checks are all ideal for freestyle stitching.

LINEN

FELT

SILK
TAFFETA

STRIPED
TICKING

HARDANGER
FABRIC

COTTON
GINGHAM

WOVEN BANDS
Narrow strips of fabric with decorative woven edges, such as this natural linen band, are available in various widths.

THREADS

Embroidery threads come in myriad colors and a broad spectrum of textures and weights. The thickness of the thread dictates the size and shape of the stitch, which will have a very different appearance if worked in a fine matt yarn or in a lustrous pearl cotton. Certain wools and threads are spun in a single strand, whilst others consist of up to six fine strands which are loosely twisted together. These can then be separated and re-combined differently, depending on the effect or line width required. The needle can be threaded with strands of two or more colors to create subtle shaded effects. Manufacturer's sample books and shade cards show the full range of different threads that are available and can be a good source of inspiration when planning a new project.

SILKS AND COTTONS

Silks and cottons are made in both single and stranded skeins. Silk, rayon, and twisted pearl cotton all have a high sheen, whilst stranded cotton gives a smooth finish. Use fine flower thread or the thicker soft cotton for a more matt appearance. Metallic threads add textural interest and silk ribbon is used for embroidering naturalistic roses and flowers.

FLOWER THREAD

STRANDED COTTON

SILK RAYON

STRANDED SILK

SILK RIBBON   **METALLIC THREAD**

PEARL COTTON

SOFT COTTON

WOOLS

The thickest wool is 4-ply tapestry, used on 10- to 14-count canvas. Use several strands of fine 2-ply crewel on canvas or a single strand on fabric. Persian has three easily separated medium-weight strands: use two or three for needlepoint and one to stitch on fabric.

SILK THREAD   **SILK THREAD**

CREWEL WOOL

TAPESTRY WOOL

PERSIAN WOOL

NEEDLES

The correct choice of needle is essential for any piece of embroidery or needlepoint. There are five different types used for decorative stitching, each with a particular purpose. All come in a range of thicknesses and lengths; select one that can be threaded easily and that passes smoothly through the fabric without snagging the thread.

Types of Needle

Chenille needles have sharp points, designed for working on heavy plainweave fabrics with thick threads. Blunt tapestry needles with long, oval eyes are used with evenweave fabric and canvas, interlacing, and for all pulled fabric and drawn thread work. Versatile crewel needles are used for most embroidery stitches. They are long with easily-threaded eyes which take one or more strands. Sharps are mainly used for hand-sewing but, like betweens, they are ideal for fine stitching and French knots.

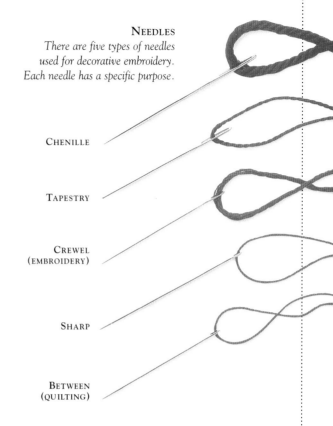

NEEDLES
There are five types of needles used for decorative embroidery. Each needle has a specific purpose.

CHENILLE

TAPESTRY

CREWEL
(EMBROIDERY)

SHARP

BETWEEN
(QUILTING)

PREPARING THE THREAD

A length of thread can be easily unwound from a reel, but care must be taken when working with cotton or wools that come in individual skeins. Twisted skeins have to be undone before they can be used, but the paper bands should not be removed from looped skeins or they will become tangled. To prevent the thread becoming damaged as it passes repeatedly through the fabric, cut off a working length of no more than 20in (50cm). Use a needle threader with fine cotton and silk or the loop method of threading (see below) for stranded and pearl threads or wool.

Keep slip knot loose

UNTYING A TWISTED SKEIN
Remove the paper bands. Untwist the skein and cut through the threads, then tie them together with a loose slip knot.

Pull thread out gently

USING A LOOPED SKEIN
Leave the bands in place. Hold one end of the skein firmly and draw out the loose thread to the required length.

Guide thread through eye

THREADING A NEEDLE
Fold thread over needle and hold the loop between thumb and finger. Slide the loop off; pass it through the eye.

FRAMES

Small-scale projects and some needlepoint can be stitched in the hand, but most embroidery has to be worked on a frame to achieve the best result. The frame maintains the fabric at an even tension and holds the grain straight, which keeps the stitches regular and even, and protects the work by reducing the amount of handling it undergoes. The choice of frame depends on both the scale of a project and the fabric being used, but is very often a personal preference. There are three basic types: fixed stretchers and adjustable scroll frames which are used for embroidery fabrics and all weights of canvas, and round hoops for cotton and linen. All of these are available with integral or additional stand attachments, which give the advantage of freeing up both hands for stitching. Larger embroideries in particular are manageable if worked on a free-standing frame. Any frame should be large enough to accommodate the whole design area; moving fabric within a frame can damage the stitches.

ROUND FRAMES

Wooden hoop frames range in diameter from 5 to 13in (12.5 to 32cm) and are ideal for smaller pieces of embroidery worked on fabric. They are light, portable and easily held in one hand, but free-standing versions, which can be clamped on to a table, are also available.

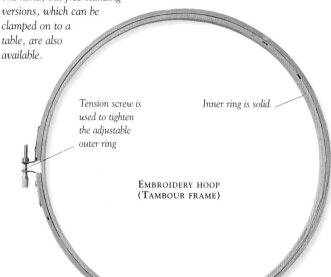

Tension screw is used to tighten the adjustable outer ring

Inner ring is solid

EMBROIDERY HOOP
(TAMBOUR FRAME)

SQUARE AND RECTANGULAR FRAMES

These can be used for canvas or embroidery fabric. Stretcher frames are sold as two pairs of struts which can be chosen and assembled to fit a particular piece of work. Scroll frames come in several widths, depending on the roller length.

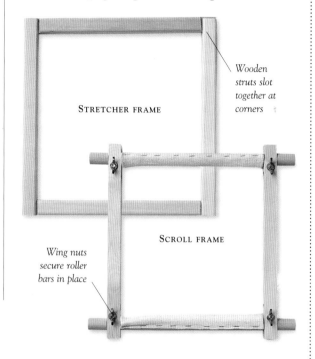

STRETCHER FRAME

Wooden struts slot together at corners

SCROLL FRAME

Wing nuts secure roller bars in place

PREPARING THE INNER RING

To prevent delicate fabrics from becoming damaged and to stop them slipping within the hoop, bind the inner ring tightly with narrow cotton tape or bias binding. Stitch the two ends together to secure.

Mounting Techniques

IT IS WORTH taking time at the outset of a project to prepare and mount the fabric properly. Neaten the edges to prevent them fraying or snagging by working a narrow hem or a machine zigzag stitch around linen and cotton fabrics, or by binding canvas with masking tape. Use a steam iron to press the fabric and remove any creases.

> ············· HANDY TIP ·············
> *Before mounting the fabric, fold it into quarters and work two rows of tacking along the creases, following the weave. Keep these lines straight to make sure that the fabric grain does not become distorted when stretched in the frame.*

USING AN EMBROIDERY HOOP
The fabric should be at least 3in (8cm) larger all around than the diameter of the hoop. Loosen the screw slightly before mounting.

MOUNTING THE FABRIC
Center the fabric over the inner ring, then gently push the outer ring over the fabric, keeping the grain straight. Tighten the screw to hold the frame together.

PREPARING A STRETCHER FRAME
The neatened fabric or canvas should be the same size as the frame. Use drawing pins or a staple gun to fix the fabric in place.

PINNING CANVAS
Mark the middle of each strut; line the canvas up to these four points. Pin from the center out towards each corner, spacing the pins at regular intervals.

SETTING UP A SCROLL FRAME
Cut the fabric or canvas to the same width as the webbing. If it is longer than the struts, any surplus can be wrapped round the bottom roller and adjusted as work progresses.

1 *Neaten the side edges. Match the midpoints of the canvas and webbing, then tack together. Sewing outwards from the center, work herringbone stitch (see p.52) over the join.*

2 *Slot the rollers into the spaces in the struts. Tighten the two top screws; then turn the bottom roller to stretch the fabric. Secure the other screws; then lace the fabric tightly over the edges using thin string and a tapestry needle.*

Stitching Techniques

T HE KEY TO a professional finish for any piece of
needlework is to keep the length of the stitches
regular and to maintain even tension throughout, whether
or not the fabric is mounted on a frame. Take time to sew
a small sample piece before embarking on any new
project, becoming familiar with the sitiches and
establishing a rhythmic pattern of working. Embroidery
stitches are constructed either vertically, usually from top
to bottom, or horizontally towards the left or right,
although they may appear at any angle in the finished
piece. Needlepoint fillings, which form all-over patterns,
are worked in diagonal, horizontal, or vertical rows.

BEGINNING TO STITCH
Follow one of the two techniques shown below
to start off or to join a new length of thread.
Both will help to guarantee that the reverse
side of the stitching is as neat as the front.

FASTENING OFF A THREAD
Fasten off the thread when it is no less than
4in (10cm) long. Try not to finish too many
threads in the same area since this can create
an uneven surface, especially in needlepoint.

LOST KNOT METHOD
*Use this technique for needlepoint and
open embroidery stitches. Knot one end
of the thread and insert the needle from
the front, a short distance along the
line to be worked. Continue stitching
so the thread is held down at the back
by the first stitches. Cut off the knot.*

RUNNING STITCH METHOD
*Use when working embroidery stitches
which are spaced closely together and
for needlepoint. Leaving a loose end of
thread at the back, work a few small
running stitches, and stitch over them.
The end can then be darned through
the reverse of the stitches.*

FASTENING OFF
*Take the needle through to the wrong
side of the fabric and turn the work
over. Pass the needle under the loops at
the back of the final few stitches for a
distance of about 1in (2.5cm), then
clip the end of the thread close to the
fabric surface.*

WAYS OF WORKING

Holding the fabric in the hand is a familiar sewing technique and some stitches, including looped embroidery stitches, are best worked this way. When the fabric is mounted in a frame, a special two-handed technique is used.

Embroidering in the Hand

Support the area being worked over the fore-finger. Hold the needle in the other hand and slide it in and out in a single movement.

LOOPED STITCHES

Loop the thread from one side to the other and use the free thumb to hold it down. Pull the needle through over the working thread. The step-by-step diagrams will indicate the point where the thread should be held.

Using Both Hands

Working with a free-standing frame may prove awkward at first but, with practice, both right- and left-handed workers will find that they can stitch quickly and evenly with two hands.

STABBING TECHNIQUE

Keep one hand on either side of the frame. Push the needle down into the fabric from the top and pull it through from below. Pass it back up with this hand, and draw it through from above.

Hand-held Needlepoint

Straight, and some crossed, stitches can be worked in the hand without any problems, but diagonal stitches will cause some distortion.

STITCHING ON CANVAS

Bind the edges of the canvas and start at the far side. Keep the unworked part rolled in one hand, while stitching with the other. Be sure to keep the tension even.

WORKING NEEDLEPOINT STITCHES

Stitches on canvas are worked into the square holes between the woven threads. To avoid splitting the stitches, always try to bring the needle up through an unworked space and take it down into an already worked hole. Do not pull the yarn too tightly or the holes will become enlarged so the canvas shows through.

1 *Work the first row, then fill in the bottom corner. Start each stitch from an unworked hole and insert the needle in to the base of the stitch in the previous row.*

2 *Fill the top corner with stitches worked in the opposite direction, ending each one at the top of the last row. Use this method with the stabbing technique.*

WORKING FILLING STITCHES

Powdered, open, and solid fillings, along with most needlepoint stitches, are worked within a specific area of a design, which may be a naturalistic leaf or petal, or a more regular geometric form. The size and shape of the individual stitches have to be altered to fill the given shape. For open and solid embroidered fillings, this means that the stitches must be worked at different lengths to fit within a curved or zigzag line, or all at the same length to complete a rectangular or square motif. Powdered fillings are worked singly within an outline; their size may be varied to add extra visual interest. Diagonal needlepoint stitches, which have a regular, all-over surface pattern, require partial stitches to be worked at the edges of the shape.

NEEDLEPOINT FILLINGS

Straight, cross, and star stitches fit easily within a square, but diagonal stitches have to be adapted. Count the intersections carefully, and make partial stitches to square off the edges of the area being worked.

COUNTED THREAD AND FREESTYLE

Embroidery stitches can be worked on either evenweave or plainweave fabric. A regularly spaced effect can easily be created by counting the threads on evenweave; work between guidelines to achieve the same result with freestyle stitching on finer plainweave fabric.

OPEN AND SOLID FILLINGS

Start a leaf at the top with a short straight stitch to fill in the point, then work downward, first increasing, then reducing the length of the stitches. Insert the needle just beyond the edge of the shape so the stitches hide the line.

EVENWEAVE FABRIC
Make each stitch over the same number of threads or thread intersections.

PLAINWEAVE FABRIC
Stitch between two parallel lines drawn onto the fabric with a dressmaker's pencil.

POWDERED FILLINGS

Work a fine outline stitch over the guideline to define the motif; then fill the shape with individual stitches. These can be arranged in a regular pattern or scattered randomly within the leaf.

TIE STITCHES

These short stitches are used to anchor looped stitches such as chain stitch, in couching, and to bunch together groups of straight stitches.

MAKING A TIE STITCH
Bring the needle up above the long stitch or inside the loop and insert it just below the thread.

WORKING OPENWORK STITCHES

In all types of openwork the background fabric is as important as the stitches themselves, and forms an integral part of the finished piece. It has to be carefully prepared for drawn thread work and for insertion (faggoting) stitches.

Drawn Thread Stitches

The open spaces that give drawn thread work its characteristic lacy appearance are formed by removing some of the woven threads that make up the fabric.

PULLING OUT THE THREADS

Evenweave cotton or linen are the best fabrics to work with. Use the point of a needle to lift up the threads and pull out enough to make an open band or bands of the required width.

Insertion Stitches

To make sure that the space between the two hems remains constant and the stitches are worked regularly, the fabric being joined has to be stitched on to paper before starting.

MOUNTING THE FABRIC

Stitch a narrow hem along each long edge. Draw two parallel lines, ¼in (6mm) apart on to a strip of heavy paper. With the right sides facing, tack one piece of fabric along each line.

FINISHING OFF

When the final stitches have been completed, take the work off the frame. Press embroidery lightly on the wrong side before mounting.

Blocking

A piece of needlepoint which incorporates diagonal stitches will inevitably become pulled out of shape as it is worked. Any distortion can be remedied by blocking the canvas.

HOW TO BLOCK

Make a template of the finished piece and mark into quarters. Tape to a board and cover with polythene. Place the dampened work face down. Match the center top edge to the template and pin. Stretch and pin the bottom edge and two sides. Insert more pins at 1in (2.5cm) intervals. Allow to dry.

Mounting

If a project is to be framed it should first be mounted on to board to keep it in shape, whether it is worked on fabric or canvas.

1 *Cut the board to size and mark into quarters. Center it on the wrong side of the fabric and fold back long edges. Pin them to the card from the center out.*

2 *Using strong thread, lace the edges together. Do the same with the other two sides. Check the fabric is centered, then tighten up and secure the threads.*

GALLERY OF STITCHES

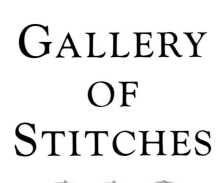

BRINGS TOGETHER ALL THE STITCHES
WORKED IN THE BOOK INTO AN EASY
REFERENCE CHAPTER

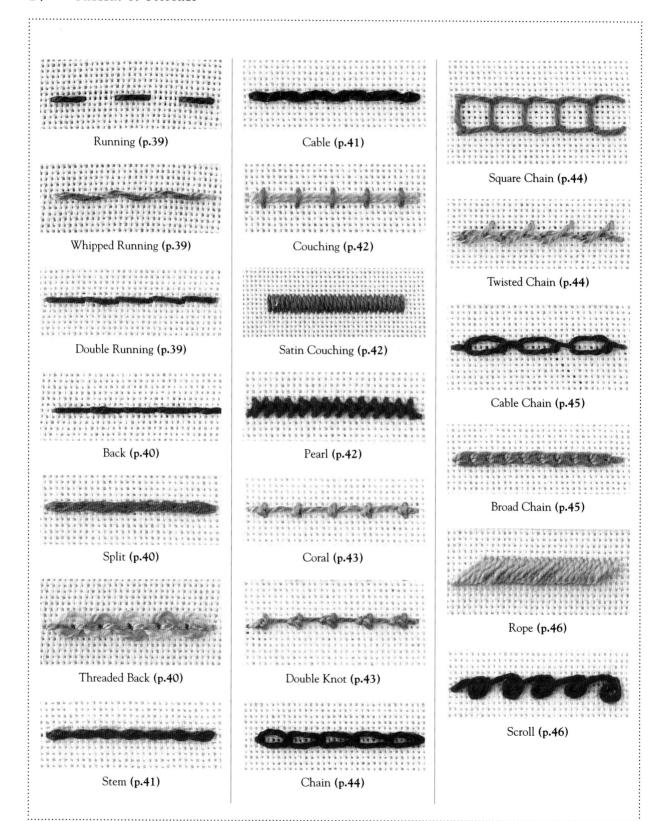

Running **(p.39)**

Whipped Running **(p.39)**

Double Running **(p.39)**

Back **(p.40)**

Split **(p.40)**

Threaded Back **(p.40)**

Stem **(p.41)**

Cable **(p.41)**

Couching **(p.42)**

Satin Couching **(p.42)**

Pearl **(p.42)**

Coral **(p.43)**

Double Knot **(p.43)**

Chain **(p.44)**

Square Chain **(p.44)**

Twisted Chain **(p.44)**

Cable Chain **(p.45)**

Broad Chain **(p.45)**

Rope **(p.46)**

Scroll **(p.46)**

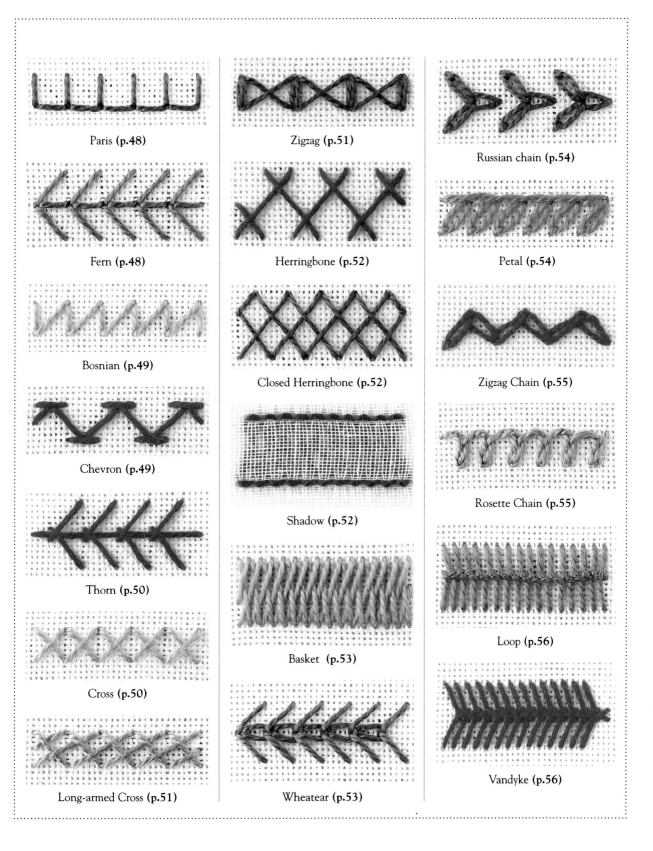

Paris (p.48)

Zigzag (p.51)

Russian chain (p.54)

Fern (p.48)

Herringbone (p.52)

Petal (p.54)

Bosnian (p.49)

Closed Herringbone (p.52)

Zigzag Chain (p.55)

Chevron (p.49)

Shadow (p.52)

Rosette Chain (p.55)

Thorn (p.50)

Basket (p.53)

Loop (p.56)

Cross (p.50)

Long-armed Cross (p.51)

Wheatear (p.53)

Vandyke (p.56)

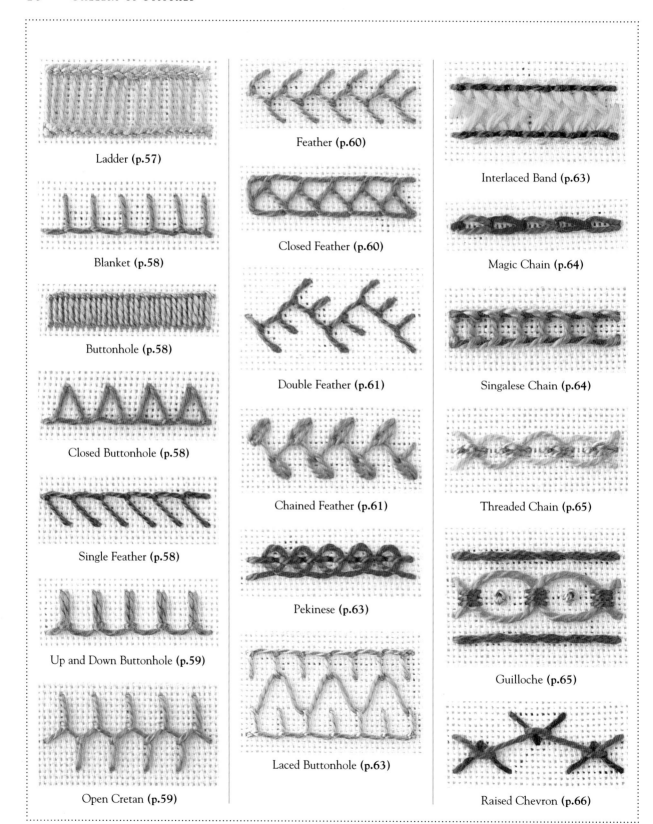

Ladder (p.57)

Blanket (p.58)

Buttonhole (p.58)

Closed Buttonhole (p.58)

Single Feather (p.58)

Up and Down Buttonhole (p.59)

Open Cretan (p.59)

Feather (p.60)

Closed Feather (p.60)

Double Feather (p.61)

Chained Feather (p.61)

Pekinese (p.63)

Laced Buttonhole (p.63)

Interlaced Band (p.63)

Magic Chain (p.64)

Singalese Chain (p.64)

Threaded Chain (p.65)

Guilloche (p.65)

Raised Chevron (p.66)

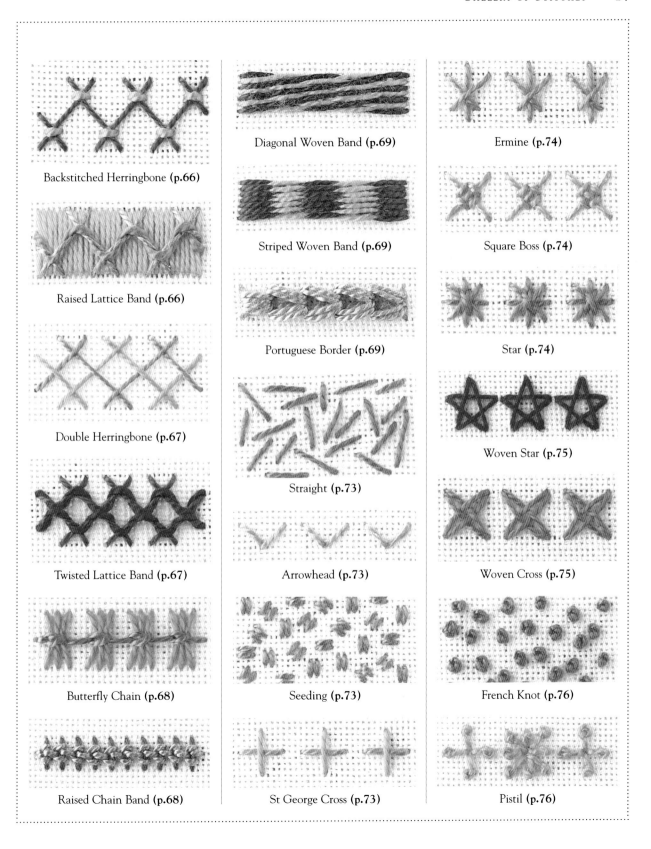

Backstitched Herringbone (p.66)

Raised Lattice Band (p.66)

Double Herringbone (p.67)

Twisted Lattice Band (p.67)

Butterfly Chain (p.68)

Raised Chain Band (p.68)

Diagonal Woven Band (p.69)

Striped Woven Band (p.69)

Portuguese Border (p.69)

Straight (p.73)

Arrowhead (p.73)

Seeding (p.73)

St George Cross (p.73)

Ermine (p.74)

Square Boss (p.74)

Star (p.74)

Woven Star (p.75)

Woven Cross (p.75)

French Knot (p.76)

Pistil (p.76)

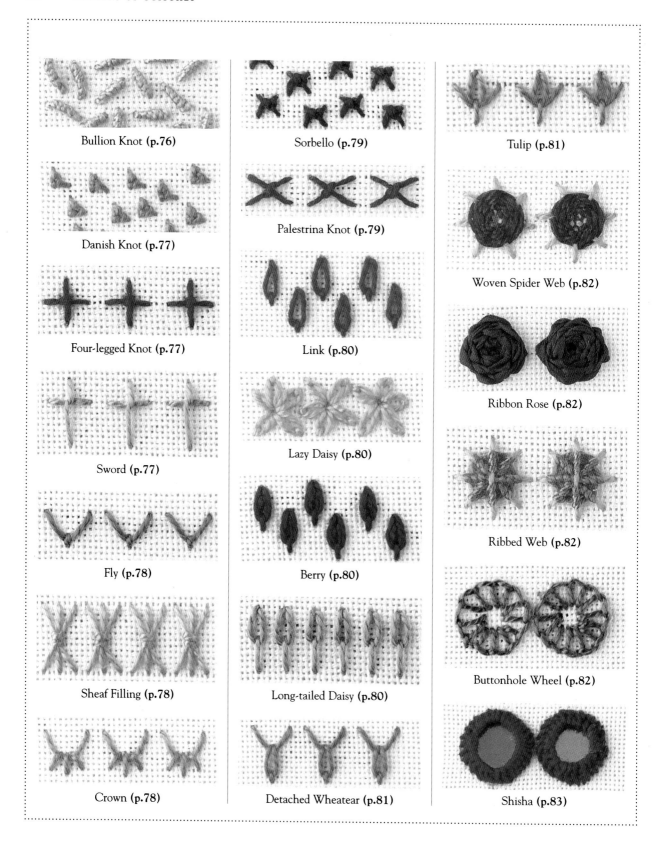

Bullion Knot (p.76)

Danish Knot (p.77)

Four-legged Knot (p.77)

Sword (p.77)

Fly (p.78)

Sheaf Filling (p.78)

Crown (p.78)

Sorbello (p.79)

Palestrina Knot (p.79)

Link (p.80)

Lazy Daisy (p.80)

Berry (p.80)

Long-tailed Daisy (p.80)

Detached Wheatear (p.81)

Tulip (p.81)

Woven Spider Web (p.82)

Ribbon Rose (p.82)

Ribbed Web (p.82)

Buttonhole Wheel (p.82)

Shisha (p.83)

Damask Darning (p.85)

Double Darning (p.85)

Brick and Cross Filling (p.85)

Satin (p.86)

Surface Satin (p.86)

Encroaching Satin (p.86)

Long and Short (p.87)

Buttonhole Filling (p.87)

Stem Filling (p.87)

Leaf (p.88)

Open Fishbone (p.88)

Attached Fly (p.89)

Close Fly (p.89)

Cretan (p.89)

Close Cretan (p.89)

Romanian Couching (p.90)

Bokhara Couching (p.90)

Spiral Couching (p.90)

Couched Filling (p.91)

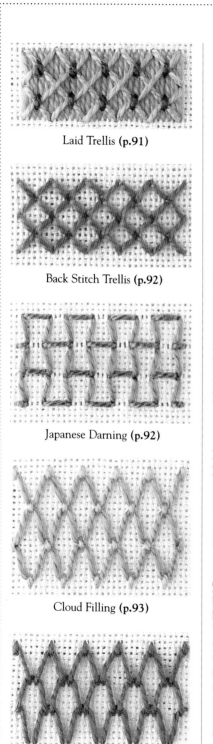

Laid Trellis (p.91)

Back Stitch Trellis (p.92)

Japanese Darning (p.92)

Cloud Filling (p.93)

Wave Filling (p.93)

Window Filling (p.97)

Pulled Wave Filling (p.97)

Three-sided (p.97)

Honeycomb Filling (p.98)

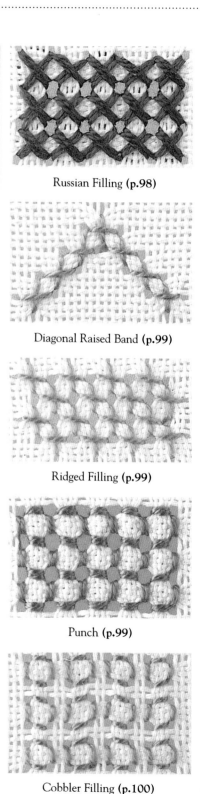

Russian Filling (p.98)

Diagonal Raised Band (p.99)

Ridged Filling (p.99)

Punch (p.99)

Cobbler Filling (p.100)

Step **(p.100)**

Outlined Diamond Eyelet **(p.103)**

Four-sided **(p.106)**

Mosaic Filling **(p.101)**

Hem **(p.105)**

Chevron Border **(p.107)**

Diagonal Satin Filling **(p.101)**

Ladder Hem **(p.105)**

Diamond Border **(p.107)**

Ringed Back Stitch Filling **(p.102)**

Serpentine Hem **(p.105)**

Laced Insertion **(p.108)**

Antique Hem **(p.105)**

Insertion Bundles **(p.108)**

Algerian Eye **(p.102)**

Italian Border **(p.106)**

Cretan Insertion **(p.108)**

Knotted Insertion (p.109)

Buttonhole Insertion
(p.109)

Needleweaving Bars
(p.110)

Zigzag Clusters (p.110)

Corded Clusters (p.110)

Antwerp Edging (p.112)

Sailor Edging (p.112)

Looped Edge (p.113)

Half Chevron (p.113)

Scalloped Edge
(p.114)

Ring Picot Edge (p.114)

Buttonhole Eyelet
(p.115)

Overcast Eyelet (p.115)

Square Eyelet (p.115)

Upright Gobelin (p.119)

Gobelin Filling (p.119)

Parisian (p.119)

Hungarian (p.120)

Hungarian Diamond
(p.120)

Single Twill (p.121)

Double Twill (p.121)

Bargello (**p.121**)

Chevron (**p.122**)

Hungarian Ground (**p.122**)

Straight Cushion (**p.123**)

Scottish Diamond (**p.123**)

Diamond (**p.124**)

Long Stitch Triangles
(**p.124**)

Lozenge (**p.125**)

Straight Milanese (**p.125**)

Double Brick (**p.126**)

Brick Filling (**p.126**)

Long and Short Brick (**p.127**)

Basket Filling (**p.127**)

Half Cross (**p.129**)

Basketweave Tent (**p.129**)

Tent (**p.129**)

Trammed Tent (**p.129**)

Gobelin (**p.130**)

Encroaching Gobelin
(**p.130**)

Reversed Sloping Gobelin
(**p.131**)

Canvas Stem (**p.131**)

Florence (**p.132**)

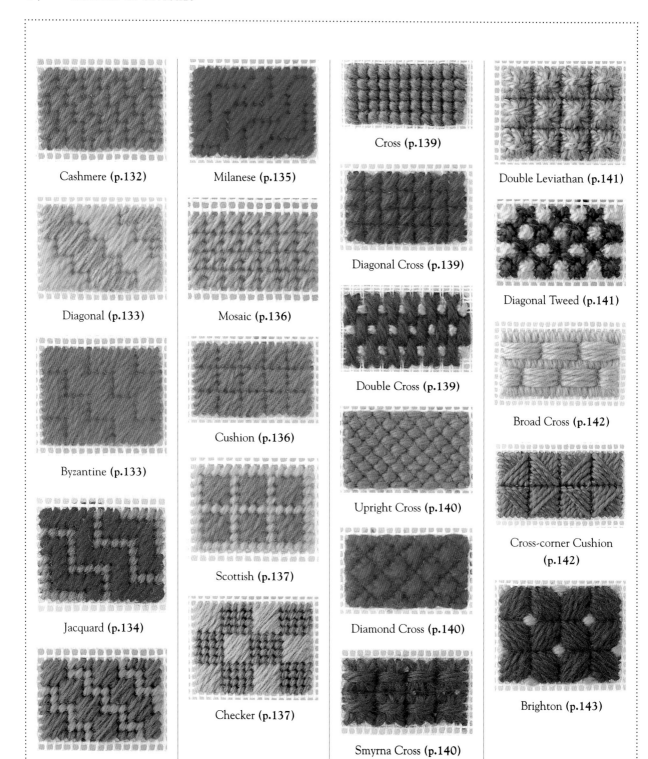

Cashmere (p.132)

Milanese (p.135)

Cross (p.139)

Double Leviathan (p.141)

Diagonal (p.133)

Mosaic (p.136)

Diagonal Cross (p.139)

Diagonal Tweed (p.141)

Byzantine (p.133)

Cushion (p.136)

Double Cross (p.139)

Broad Cross (p.142)

Jacquard (p.134)

Scottish (p.137)

Upright Cross (p.140)

Cross-corner Cushion (p.142)

Moorish (p.135)

Checker (p.137)

Diamond Cross (p.140)

Smyrna Cross (p.140)

Brighton (p.143)

Rice (p.143)

Plaited Gobelin (p.144)

Greek (p.144)

Plait (p.145)

Fishbone (p.145)

Fern (p.146)

Fir (p.146)

Rhodes (p.147)

Half Rhodes (p.147)

Star (p.148)

Eye (p.148)

Diamond Eye (p.149)

Fan (p.149)

Rya (p.151)

Turkey (p.151)

Houndstooth (p.152)

Knitting (p.153)

Old Wheatsheaf (p.153)

Tied Gobelin (p.154)

French (p.154)

Pineapple (p.155)

Arrow (p.155)

LINE AND BORDER STITCHES

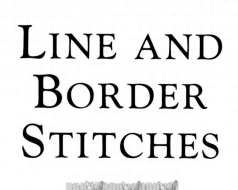

OUTLINE STITCHES

· · · · · · · ◆ · · · · · · ·

BORDER STITCHES

· · · · · · · ◆ · · · · · · ·

COMPOSITE BORDER STITCHES

Outline Stitches

THIS GROUP INCLUDES some of the most basic and versatile embroidery stitches, which are all worked continuously in a curved or straight row. They can be sewn in any thread on any fabric, depending on the effect desired, and are used to achieve fine lines and details. Use these stitches to 'draw' designs and motifs, for monograms and lettering, or to define shapes which will be completed with filling stitches. Running and back stitches provide the foundation for some composite stitches and can be interlaced with contrasting threads.

Running

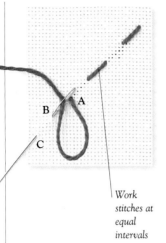

········ LEVEL ········
Easy

·········· USES ··········
*Simple lines and outlines;
basis for other stitches;
hand sewing and quilting;
reinforcement for cutwork*

······· METHOD ·······
*Regularly spaced straight
stitches of equal length*

······ MATERIALS ·······
Any fabric; any thread

*Work
stitches at
equal
intervals*

Come up at **A**, then insert the
needle at **B**. Bring it out again
at **C**. Continue, spacing the
stitches evenly and making
them all the same length.

Whipped Running

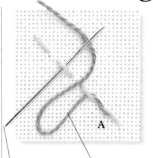

····· OTHER NAME ······
Cordonnet stitch

·········· LEVEL ··········
Easy

·········· USES ··········
Straight or curved outlines

······· METHOD ········
Laced running stitch

······· MATERIALS ·······
*Any fabric; any two
threads – contrasting
colors and thicknesses for
greater effect; blunt needle
for whipping*

*Use blunt needle
to avoid catching
threads*

*Do not pull
lacing thread
tightly*

Work a foundation of closely
spaced running stitch (see
left). Using a blunt needle,
bring the second thread up at
A. Slide the needle under the
next stitch from right to left
and pull through gently.
Continue whipping to the
end of the line.

Double Running

····· OTHER NAMES ·····
*Holbein stitch;
Assisi stitch*

·········· LEVEL ··········
Easy

·········· USES ··········
*With cross stitch; in Assisi
and Blackwork
(Spanish work)*

······· METHOD ·········
*Counted thread stitch
worked with two rows of
running stitch*

······ MATERIALS ·······
*Evenweave fabric; any
embroidery thread*

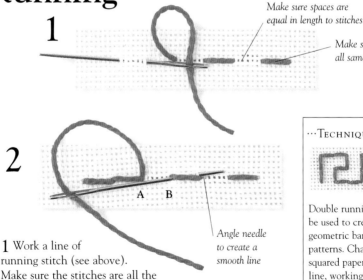

1

*Make sure spaces are
equal in length to stitches*

*Make stitches
all same length*

2

*Angle needle
to create a
smooth line*

1 Work a line of
running stitch (see above).
Make sure the stitches are all the
same length, and equal in length to the spaces.

2 Fill in the spaces on the return journey. Come out at the
top of the previous stitch, at **A**. Insert the needle just below
the start of the next stitch at **B**. Repeat to the end of the row.

··· TECHNIQUE VARIATION ···

Double running stitch can
be used to create intricate
geometric bands and filling
patterns. Chart the design on
squared paper. Stitch along the
line, working every other
stitch. On the return journey,
fill in the spaces with a second
row of running stitch worked in
the opposite direction.

Back

········ LEVEL ········
Easy

········ USES ········
*Details and fine outlines,
lettering, basis for other
composite stitches*

······ MATERIALS ······
*Any fabric; any thread –
untwisted threads give
smooth effect*

*Make sure B and C
are equidistant from A*

Come up at **A**. Insert the
needle at **B**, then bring it out
again one stitch length ahead
of **A** at **C**. Insert the needle
again at **A** and continue
making regular backward
stitches in the same way.

Split

········ LEVEL ········
Easy

········ USES ········
*Outlines; in close rows as
filling; padded edge for
solid filling stitches*

······ MATERIALS ······
*Any fabric; soft,
untwisted thread such as
stranded cotton or silk
floss; sharp needle*

*Use sharp
needle to
divide thread
easily*

*Keep stitches
regular to
create smooth
surface*

Come up at **A** and work a
straight stitch across to **B**.
Bring the needle up at **C**, half-
way along the stitch, so that it
splits the thread. Pull through.
Insert the needle at **D** and
repeat to continue.

Threaded Back

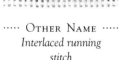

····· OTHER NAME ·····
*Interlaced running
stitch*

········ LEVEL ········
Easy

········ USES ········
*Flexible, decorative
outlines and borders*

········ METHOD ········
*Row of back stitch
interlaced with one or
two threads*

······ MATERIALS ······
*Any fabric; two or three
colors of any thick
embroidery thread;
blunt needle*

1

*Do not
pull thread
too tightly*

*Use blunt needle to
avoid catching threads*

2

*Keep loops even
on both sides*

1 Work a foundation of back stitch (see above).
Bring the second thread up at **A**. Slide the needle
under the next stitch, then pass it back under the
following stitch. Continue weaving from side to side.

2 Take the thread down at **B** and finish off. For a
double-threaded variation bring another thread up at **C**
and weave in the same way as before, filling in the gaps.

Stem

····· OTHER NAMES ·····
Outline stitch;
crewel stitch

·········· LEVEL ··········
Easy

·········· USES ··········
Outlines; flower stems;
worked in rows as filling

······ MATERIALS ······
Any fabric;
any embroidery thread
or crewel wool

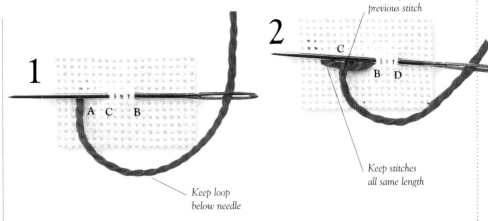

Keep loop
below needle

Make sure thread
comes up above
previous stitch

Keep stitches
all same length

1 Start at **A**, then insert the needle at **B**. Bring the needle up in the center at **C**.

2 Insert the needle at **D** and bring it out at the end of the previous stitch, at **B**. Continue making a row of overlapping stitches.

·········· TECHNIQUE VARIATION ··········

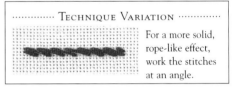

For a more solid, rope-like effect, work the stitches at an angle.

Cable

····· OTHER NAMES ·····
Alternating stem stitch;
side-to-side stem stitch

·········· LEVEL ··········
Easy

·········· USES ··········
Straight and curved
outlines; narrow border

······ MATERIALS ······
Any fabric;
any embroidery thread

Keep loop
below needle

Keep loop
above needle

Make sure E and B
are equidistant from D

1 Start at **A**, then insert the needle at **B**. Bring the needle up in the center at **C** and pull through.

2 Insert the needle at **D** and bring it back up at **B**.

3 Keeping the loop below the needle, insert at **E** and come up again at **D**. Repeat steps 2 and 3 to continue stitching.

Couching

····· OTHER NAME ·····
Laid thread

········ LEVEL ········
Easy

········· USES ·········
*Straight and curved
outlines; metal thread
work; in rows as filling*

······METHOD······
*Laid threads held down
with small tie stitches*

······ MATERIALS ······
*Any closely woven fabric;
thick or delicate embroidery
threads; finer thread for
couching; frame*

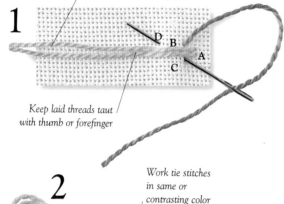

*Vary number of laid threads depending
on thickness of line required*

*Keep laid threads taut
with thumb or forefinger*

*Work tie stitches
in same or
contrasting color*

1 Bring the main threads out at
A and lay them along the line to
be worked. To make the tie
stitches (see p.20), come up at **B**
using the couching thread. Insert
the needle at **C**, over the laid
threads, and bring it out at **D** to
start the next stitch.

2 Continue working evenly
spaced tie stitches over the laid
thread to the end of the line.
Finish off all threads at the back.

·········STITCH VARIATION·········

Satin couching,
known also as
trailing stitch,
is a variation
of couching, in which the tie stitches are
worked very closely together so that the laid
thread is completely covered.

Pearl

········ LEVEL ·········
Intermediate

········· USES ·········
*Intricate or straight
outlines; monograms*

········ METHOD ·········
*Knotted stitch, worked in
continuous line*

······ MATERIALS ·······
*Any fabric; thick, non-
stranded embroidery
thread*

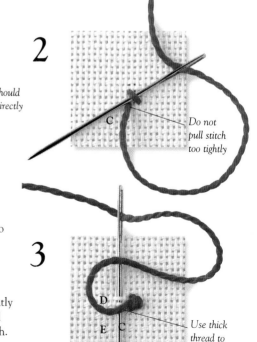

*Needle should
emerge directly
below B*

*Do not
pull stitch
too tightly*

*Use thick
thread to
create raised
knot*

1 Start at **A** and make a diagonal stitch up to
B. Bring the needle out at **C**.

2 Pull the thread to form a loop. Slide the
needle under the stitch from right to left.

3 Tighten the knot by pulling the thread gently
downward. Take the needle up to the left and
insert at **D** to form the loop for the next stitch.
Come out at **E**. Repeat steps 2 and 3 to
continue along the row.

Coral

····· OTHER NAMES ·····
*Knotted stitch; snail trail;
beaded stitch*

·········· LEVEL ··········
Easy

··········· USES ···········
*Straight and curved
outlines; in rows as
textured filling*

········ METHOD ········
*Series of closely or widely
spaced single knots*

······· MATERIALS ·······
*Any fabric; thick,
non-stranded thread*

1

*Hold down thread with
thumb or forefinger*

*Thread loop
should lie
under needle*

2

3

*Keep needle at
right angle to line*

1 Start at **A** and hold the thread down along the stitching line. Insert the needle at **B** and loop the thread from left to right. Bring the point out over the loop at **C**.

2 Pull the needle gently through the loop so that the thread tightens into a knot.

3 Take the needle across to the left and insert it at **D**. Bring it out at **E**, ready for the next knot. Repeat steps 1 and 2 to continue.

Double Knot

····· OTHER NAMES ·····
*Old English knot stitch;
Palestrina stitch;
Smyrna stitch*

·········· LEVEL ··········
Intermediate

········ METHOD ········
*Knotted stitch, worked in
continuous line*

··········· USES ···········
Outlines and borders

······· MATERIALS ·······
*Any fabric; thick,
non-stranded
embroidery thread*

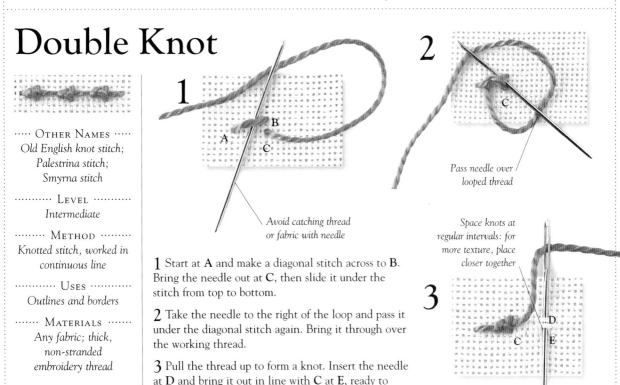

1

*Avoid catching thread
or fabric with needle*

2

*Pass needle over
looped thread*

*Space knots at
regular intervals: for
more texture, place
closer together*

3

1 Start at **A** and make a diagonal stitch across to **B**. Bring the needle out at **C**, then slide it under the stitch from top to bottom.

2 Take the needle to the right of the loop and pass it under the diagonal stitch again. Bring it through over the working thread.

3 Pull the thread up to form a knot. Insert the needle at **D** and bring it out in line with **C** at **E**, ready to work the next stitch.

Chain

····· OTHER NAMES ·····
point de chainette;
tambour stitch

·········· LEVEL ··········
Easy

·········· USES ··········
*Straight lines and curves;
lettering; in rows
or spiral as filling*

·········METHOD·········
*Looped stitch, worked
from top to bottom*

······ MATERIALS ·······
Any fabric; any thread

1

*Take needle back
into hole from
which it emerged*

A

B

*Hold loop
down with
thumb or
forefinger*

2

*Do not
pull
thread
tightly*

B

C

3

*Make
loops
all
same
length*

C

D

E

1 Start at **A**. Loop the thread from left to right and insert the needle again at **A**. Bring it through over the working thread at **B**.

2 Repeat step 1 to make the second stitch. Insert the needle inside the first loop at **B** and bring it out at **C**.

3 When the final stitch has been made, finish off by anchoring the last loop down with a small tie stitch (see p.20) from **D** to **E**.

Square Chain

····· OTHER NAMES ·····
*Ladder stitch; Roman
chain; open chain stitch*

·········· LEVEL ··········
Easy

·········· USES ··········
*Broad outlines; couching
stitch; foundation for
ribbon decoration;
traditional Indian
embroidery*

········· METHOD ·········
*Looped stitch, worked
from top to bottom*

······ MATERIALS ·······
Any fabric; any thread

A   B

C

*Keep thread
loose*

Come out at **A**. Insert the needle inside the previous loop at **B**. Bring it through over the working thread at **C**, leaving an open loop. Repeat to continue. Anchor the final loop with a tie stitch (see p.20) at each corner.

Twisted Chain

·········· LEVEL ··········
Easy

·········· USES ··········
*Curved and textured
outlines*

········· METHOD ·········
*Chain stitch variation
with crossed loop*

······ MATERIALS ·······
*Any fabric; any thread –
non-stranded threads
give best effect*

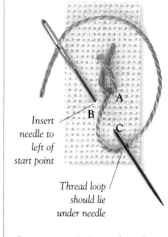

A

B

C

*Insert
needle to
left of
start point*

*Thread loop
should lie
under needle*

Come up at **A**. Loop thread from left to right, insert the needle at **B**. Come up at **C**, pull through over the working thread. Repeat to continue. Finish with a tie stitch (see p.20) over the final loop.

Cable Chain

·········· LEVEL ··········
Intermediate

········ METHOD ········
*Looped and twisted stitch,
worked from top
to bottom*

············ USES ············
*Decorative straight or
curved outlines*

······· MATERIALS ·······
*Any fabric; any thick
embroidery thread*

*Hold thread
to keep it taut*

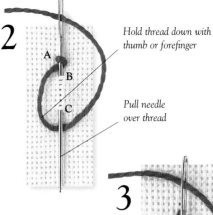

*Hold thread down with
thumb or forefinger*

*Pull needle
over thread*

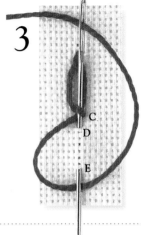

1 Start at **A**. Wrap the thread over and under the needle from left to right.

2 Insert the needle at **B**. Bring the point out at **C**, over the working thread. Pull the needle through to form the first two links.

3 Twist the thread around the needle again and work the next stitch from **D** to **E**. Repeat steps 1 and 2 to continue stitching downward.

Broad Chain

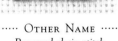

····· OTHER NAME ·····
Reversed chain stitch

·········· LEVEL ··········
Intermediate

········ METHOD ········
*Looped stitch, worked
from top to bottom*

··········· USES ···········
Solid, flexible outline

······· MATERIALS ·······
*Any fabric;
firm embroidery thread;*

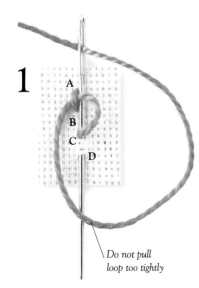

*Do not pull
loop too tightly*

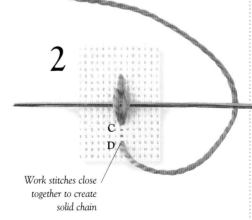

*Work stitches close
together to create
solid chain*

1 Start at **A** and make a short upright stitch to **B**. Come out directly below **B** at **C**, and slide the needle under the upright stitch from right to left. Take it down at **C**, pulling the thread gently to form the first loop. Bring the needle out again at **D**.

2 Pass the needle under both sides of the loop, then take it down at **D**. Repeat from **C** to continue.

Rope

·········· LEVEL ··········
Advanced

·········· USES ···········
Straight, curved or spiral outlines

········ MATERIALS ········
Any fabric; any thick thread – stranded cotton gives a smooth effect; frame

·········· TIP ············
Vary the angle of the stitches to work around a curve

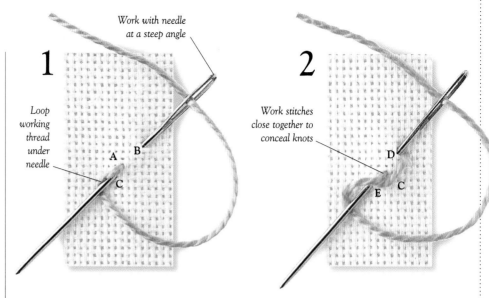

Work with needle at a steep angle

Loop working thread under needle

Work stitches close together to conceal knots

1 Start at **A**. Take the needle diagonally across and insert at **B**, then bring it up below and to the left of **A**, at **C**.

2 Pull the needle over the working thread to form a small knot at the base of the stitch. Insert the needle at **D** and bring it up at **E** to make the next stitch. Repeat this step to continue.

Scroll

····· OTHER NAME ·····
Single knotted line stitch

·········· LEVEL ··········
Intermediate

·········· USES ··········
Decorative outlines

········ METHOD ········
Looped knot stitch

······ MATERIALS ·······
Any fabric; firm, non-stranded embroidery thread; frame

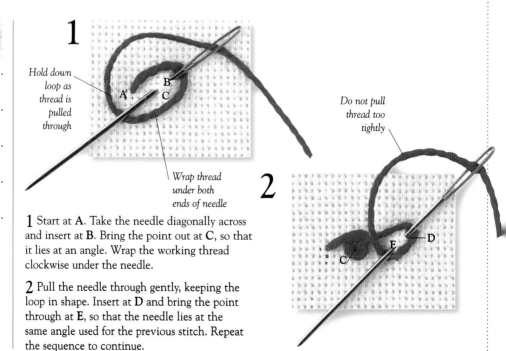

Hold down loop as thread is pulled through

Wrap thread under both ends of needle

Do not pull thread too tightly

1 Start at **A**. Take the needle diagonally across and insert at **B**. Bring the point out at **C**, so that it lies at an angle. Wrap the working thread clockwise under the needle.

2 Pull the needle through gently, keeping the loop in shape. Insert at **D** and bring the point through at **E**, so that the needle lies at the same angle used for the previous stitch. Repeat the sequence to continue.

Border Stitches

THIS IS THE largest, most widely used group of stitches and includes flat, looped, and knotted techniques. Border stitches are used to create broad, decorative straight lines, frames, and edgings. They can be worked in straight or curved rows, singly as outlines, or repeated to form a filling to cover a larger area. Use plainweave fabric for freestyle stitching or evenweave to produce the more regular stitches of counted thread work. Mount the fabric in a frame to prevent it from puckering and to keep the stitches even, especially those such as herringbone which are made up of long straight stitches.

Paris

····· OTHER NAME ·····
Open square stitch

········· LEVEL ·········
Easy

·········· USES ··········
*Light border; in rows
as filling*

········ METHOD ········
*Back stitch variation with
upright branches*

····· MATERIALS ·····
*Evenweave fabric; any
thread*

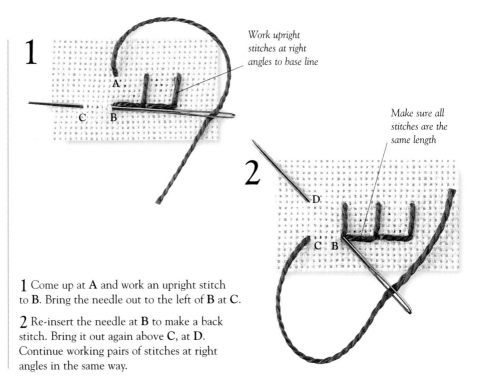

*Work upright
stitches at right
angles to base line*

*Make sure all
stitches are the
same length*

1 Come up at **A** and work an upright stitch
to **B**. Bring the needle out to the left of **B** at **C**.

2 Re-insert the needle at **B** to make a back
stitch. Bring it out again above **C**, at **D**.
Continue working pairs of stitches at right
angles in the same way.

Fern

····· OTHER NAME ·····
Fern leaf stitch

·········· LEVEL ··········
Easy

·········· USES ··········
*Leaf veins and delicate
foliage sprays*

····· MATERIALS ······
Any fabric; any thread

············ TIP ············
*Vary length of stitches
when working on a curve*

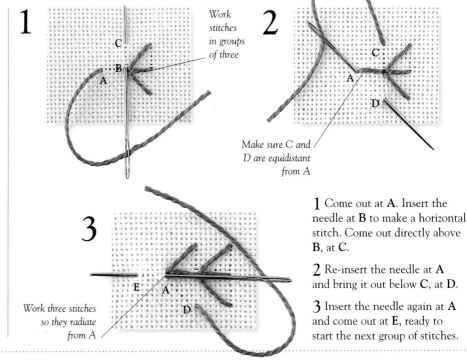

*Work
stitches
in groups
of three*

*Make sure C and
D are equidistant
from A*

*Work three stitches
so they radiate
from A*

1 Come out at **A**. Insert the
needle at **B** to make a horizontal
stitch. Come out directly above
B, at **C**.

2 Re-insert the needle at **A**
and bring it out below **C**, at **D**.

3 Insert the needle again at **A**
and come out at **E**, ready to
start the next group of stitches.

Bosnian

····· OTHER NAME ·····
Fence stitch

·········· LEVEL ··········
Easy

·········· USES ··········
*Straight borders or
outlines; in rows as filling*

········ METHOD ········
*Worked horizontally in
two journeys*

····· MATERIALS ·····
Any fabric; any thread

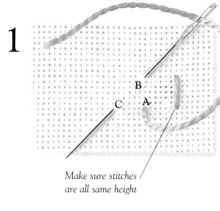

*Make sure stitches
are all same height*

*Work diagonal
stitches to form
zigzag line*

1 Come up at **A** and make an upright stitch to **B**. Bring the needle out to the left of **A**, at **C**. Continue working a row of evenly spaced straight stitches.

2 Fill the spaces with slanting stitches. Come up at **C**, insert the needle at **B**, then bring it out at **A**. Repeat to the end of the row.

Chevron

·········· LEVEL ··········
Easy

············ USES ············
*Straight border; in close
rows as light filling; in
smocking as surface
honeycomb stitch*

········ METHOD ········
*Worked horizontally
between parallel lines*

····· MATERIALS ·····
Any fabric; any thread

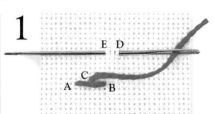

*Keep thread
above needle*

*Make sure E and F
are equidistant from D*

*Work diagonal stitches
at consistent angles*

*Make all horizontal
stitches same length*

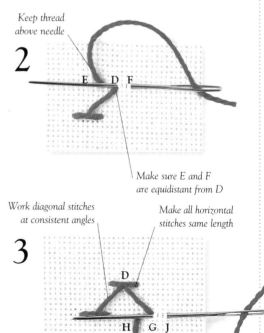

1 Start at **A** and make a horizontal straight stitch to **B**. Bring the needle out at the center of the stitch, at **C**. Take the needle up to the right and insert it at **D**, then bring it out in line with **D**, at **E**.

2 Take the needle to the right and insert it at **F**. Come out again at **D**.

3 Take the needle down and insert at **G**, then come out at **H**. Insert the needle to the right, at **J**, and bring it out again at **G**. Repeat the sequence to continue.

Thorn

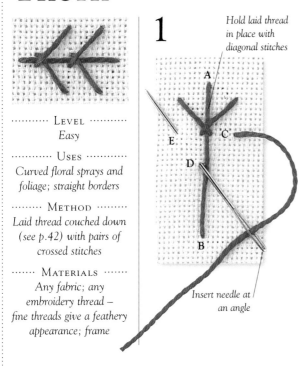

1

Hold laid thread
in place with
diagonal stitches

Insert needle at
an angle

······· LEVEL ········
Easy

········ USES ········
*Curved floral sprays and
foliage; straight borders*

······· METHOD ········
*Laid thread couched down
(see p.42) with pairs of
crossed stitches*

······ MATERIALS ·······
*Any fabric; any
embroidery thread –
fine threads give a feathery
appearance; frame*

2

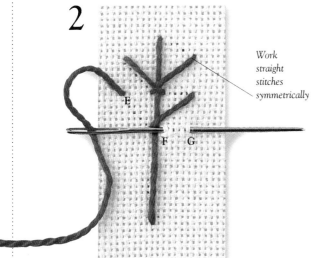

Work
straight
stitches
symmetrically

1 Start at **A** and, following the line to be worked, make a
long stitch to **B**. Use a second thread to work the couching
stitches. Come up at **C** and take the needle across the laid
thread to insert at **D**. Bring the needle out at **E**.

2 Insert the needle at **F** and bring it out at **G**, ready to
make the next diagonal stitch. Make further pairs of stitches
in the same way along the laid thread.

Cross

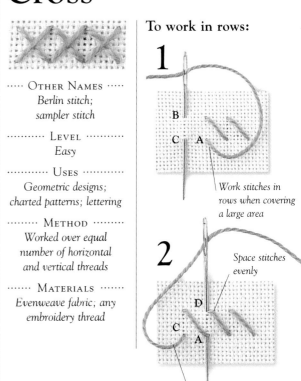

To work in rows:

1

Work stitches in
rows when covering
a large area

2

Space stitches
evenly

Make sure top stitches
all lie in same direction

······ OTHER NAMES ·····
*Berlin stitch;
sampler stitch*

········ LEVEL ·········
Easy

········ USES ·········
*Geometric designs;
charted patterns; lettering*

········ METHOD ·········
*Worked over equal
number of horizontal
and vertical threads*

······ MATERIALS ·······
*Evenweave fabric; any
embroidery thread*

1 Come up at **A**, insert the needle at **B** and come out at **C**.
Repeat to make a series of evenly spaced diagonal stitches.

2 Work the top stitches in the opposite direction. Take the
needle across from **C** and insert at **D**. Come out again at **A**.
Repeat to complete the row.

To work stitches singly:

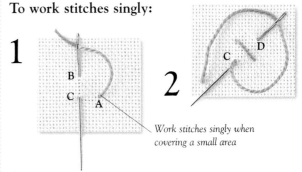

1

2

Work stitches singly when
covering a small area

1 Start at **A**. Take the needle diagonally left and insert at
B, then bring it out at **C**.

2 Insert the needle at **D** to complete the cross. Bring the
needle out at **C** to work the next stitch.

Long-armed Cross

····· OTHER NAMES ·····
Plaited Slav stitch;
long-legged cross stitch

·········· LEVEL ··········
Intermediate

·········· USES ··········
Straight frame or border;
in rows as filling

········· METHOD ·········
Cross stitch variation
worked horizontally

······ MATERIALS ······
Evenweave fabric; thick
embroidery threads –
heavier threads give a
more raised appearance

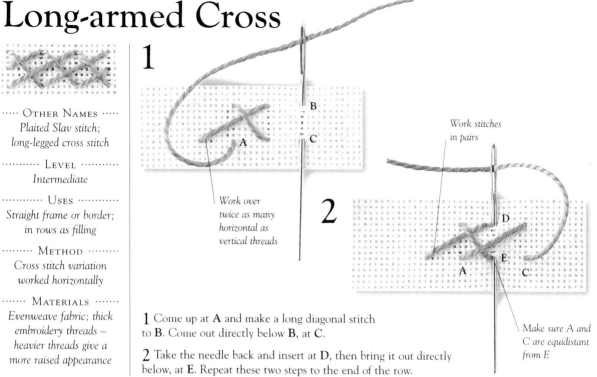

Work over
twice as many
horizontal as
vertical threads

Work stitches
in pairs

Make sure A and
C are equidistant
from E

1 Come up at **A** and make a long diagonal stitch to **B**. Come out directly below **B**, at **C**.

2 Take the needle back and insert at **D**, then bring it out directly below, at **E**. Repeat these two steps to the end of the row.

Zigzag

·········· LEVEL ··········
Easy

·········· USES ··········
Open outline; in close
rows as open filling

········· METHOD ·········
Alternate upright and
diagonal stitches, worked
horizontally in two
journeys

······ MATERIALS ······
Any fabric; any thread –
fine twisted threads give
a more open effect

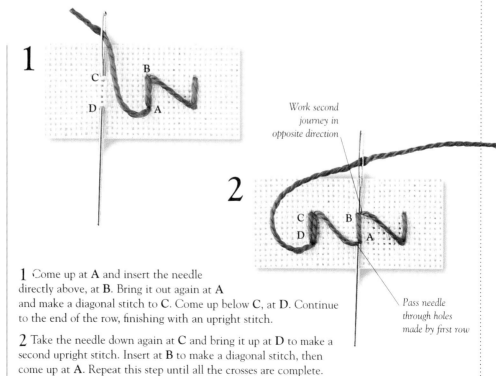

Work second
journey in
opposite direction

Pass needle
through holes
made by first row

1 Come up at **A** and insert the needle directly above, at **B**. Bring it out again at **A** and make a diagonal stitch to **C**. Come up below **C**, at **D**. Continue to the end of the row, finishing with an upright stitch.

2 Take the needle down again at **C** and bring it up at **D** to make a second upright stitch. Insert at **B** to make a diagonal stitch, then come up at **A**. Repeat this step until all the crosses are complete.

Herringbone

····· OTHER NAMES ·····
Russian cross stitch;
fishnet stitch

········· LEVEL ··········
Easy

··········· USES ···········
Decorative straight edging;
base for composite
stitches; in rows
as open filling

······ MATERIALS ······
Evenweave fabric; any
embroidery thread

Cross diagonal stitches
at top and bottom

2

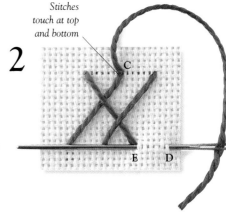

Keep stitches
spaced evenly
and equal
in length

1

1 Come up at **A**, take the needle diagonally up to **B** and insert. Bring it out at **C**, making a small back stitch.

2 Take the needle down and insert at **D**, then bring it through at **E**. Repeat these two steps to the end of the row.

Closed Herringbone

···· OTHER NAME ·····
Double back stitch

·········· LEVEL ··········
Intermediate

········· METHOD ·········
Herringbone variation

··········· USES ···········
Open border; in rows as
lattice filling

······ MATERIALS ·······
Evenweave fabric; any
thread; frame

Stitches
touch at top
and bottom

2

1

1 Come up at **A** and make a diagonal stitch across to **B**. Bring the needle out on the same level, at **C**.

2 Take the needle down to **D** and insert, then come through at **E**. Repeat these two steps to continue.

··················· STITCH VARIATION ···················

Shadow stitch is formed when closed herringbone stitch is worked on the reverse side of a semi-transparent material. The design will be outlined with back stitch and the crossed threads form a dense band of color, which shows through the fabric. Mount fabric in a frame.

Basket

·········· LEVEL ··········
Advanced

·········· USES ··········
*Straight bands and
borders; in rows as filling*

········ METHOD ········
*Alternate forward and
backward stitches, worked
downward between two
parallel lines*

······ MATERIALS ······
*Any fabric; stranded
thread gives a
smoother finish*

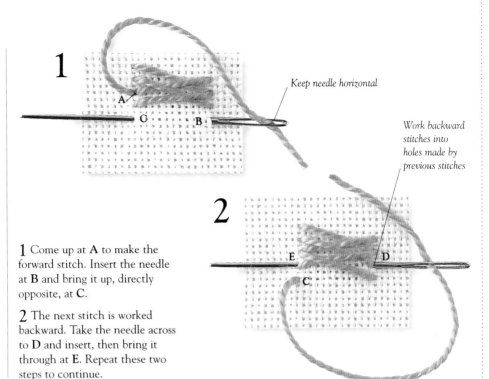

Keep needle horizontal

*Work backward
stitches into
holes made by
previous stitches*

1 Come up at **A** to make the
forward stitch. Insert the needle
at **B** and bring it up, directly
opposite, at **C**.

2 The next stitch is worked
backward. Take the needle across
to **D** and insert, then bring it
through at **E**. Repeat these two
steps to continue.

Wheatear

·········· LEVEL ··········
Intermediate

·········· USES ··········
*Straight or gently curved
outlines; traditionally
worked on smocks
and childrens' clothes;
used singly as filling
(see p.81)*

········ METHOD ········
*Looped stitch, worked
from top to bottom*

······ MATERIALS ······
*Any fabric; non-stranded
threads give raised effect*

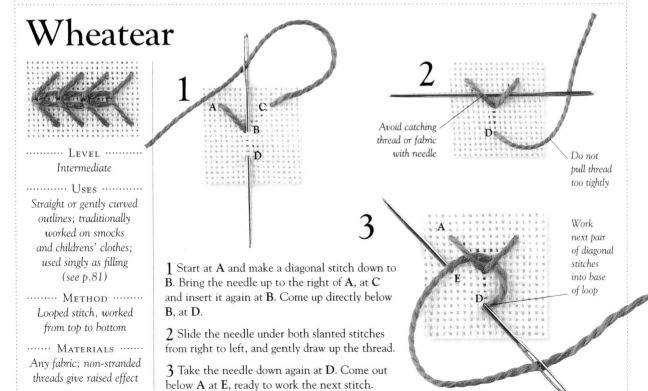

*Avoid catching
thread or fabric
with needle*

*Do not
pull thread
too tightly*

*Work
next pair
of diagonal
stitches
into base
of loop*

1 Start at **A** and make a diagonal stitch down to
B. Bring the needle up to the right of **A**, at **C**
and insert it again at **B**. Come up directly below
B, at **D**.

2 Slide the needle under both slanted stitches
from right to left, and gently draw up the thread.

3 Take the needle down again at **D**. Come out
below **A** at **E**, ready to work the next stitch.

Russian Chain

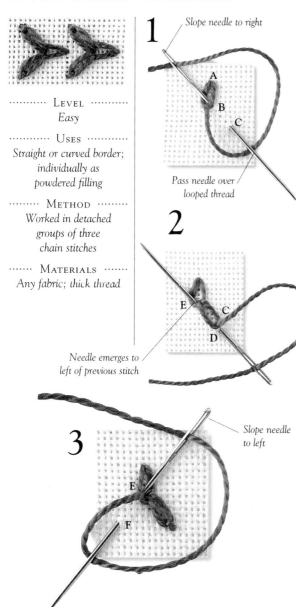

········· LEVEL ·········
Easy

········· USES ·········
Straight or curved border;
individually as
powdered filling

········· METHOD ·········
Worked in detached
groups of three
chain stitches

········· MATERIALS ·········
Any fabric; thick thread

1 Slope needle to right

Pass needle over
looped thread

A
B
C

2 Needle emerges to
left of previous stitch

E   C
D

3 Slope needle
to left

E
F

1 Work a chain stitch (see p.44) from **A** to **B**, bringing
the needle out to the right of center. Insert again at **B**, loop
the thread from left to right and bring the needle out at **C**.

2 Insert the needle at **D** to make a tie stitch (see p.20),
then bring the needle up inside the first loop, at **E**.

3 Make the third chain stitch at an angle from **E** to **F** in
the same way. Finish with a tie stitch. Work the next and
subsequent groups of stitches directly below the first.

Petal

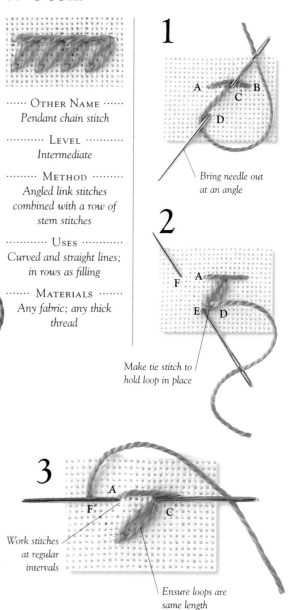

········· OTHER NAME ·········
Pendant chain stitch

········· LEVEL ·········
Intermediate

········· METHOD ·········
Angled link stitches
combined with a row of
stem stitches

········· USES ·········
Curved and straight lines;
in rows as filling

········· MATERIALS ·········
Any fabric; any thick
thread

1 Bring needle out
at an angle

A   B
C
D

2 Make tie stitch to
hold loop in place

F   A
E   D

3 Work stitches
at regular
intervals

F   A
C

Ensure loops are
same length

1 Start at **A** and make a straight stitch to **B**. Bring the
needle up at the center of the stitch at **C**. Work a chain
stitch (see p.44) from **C** to **D**.

2 Insert the needle at **E** to make a tie stitch (see p.20).
Come out to the left of **A** at **F**.

3 Insert the needle again at the top of the loop, at **C**, and
come out at **A**, ready to make the next pair of stitches.

Zigzag Chain

······ OTHER NAME ······
Vandyke chain

·········· LEVEL ··········
Intermediate

·········· USES ··········
Straight and gently curved lines and outlines

········· METHOD ·········
Chain stitches worked at alternate angles

······· MATERIALS ·······
Any fabric; twisted thread; sharp needle

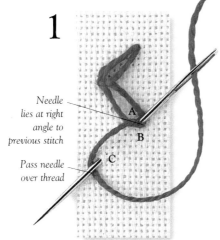

1

Needle lies at right angle to previous stitch

Pass needle over thread

2

Anchor loop to fabric with next stitch

Use sharp needle to pierce thread

1 Come up inside the previous stitch at **A**. Loop the thread from left to right and insert the needle at **B** so that it pierces the base of the stitch. Bring the needle out at **C**, over the working thread.

2 Loop the thread from right to left and insert the needle at **D**, through the base of the last stitch. Come out at **E** and continue making stitches at right angles. Finish off with a tie stitch (see p.20) over the final loop.

Rosette Chain

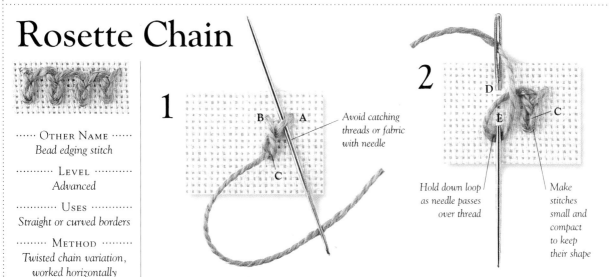

······ OTHER NAME ······
Bead edging stitch

·········· LEVEL ··········
Advanced

·········· USES ··········
Straight or curved borders

········· METHOD ·········
Twisted chain variation, worked horizontally

······· MATERIALS ·······
Any fabric; thick non-stranded thread

1

Avoid catching threads or fabric with needle

2

Hold down loop as needle passes over thread

Make stitches small and compact to keep their shape

1 Start at **A**. Loop the thread from left to right and insert the needle at **B**. Come up at **C** and pull the needle through the loop. Slide the needle under the thread to the left of **A** from bottom to top and pull through gently.

2 Insert the needle at **D** and come up through the loop at **E**, as before. Repeat to continue.

········ TECHNIQUE VARIATION ········

Work rosette chain in a circle to create a petalled flower motif. The stitches radiate from a central point and should be evenly spaced.

Loop

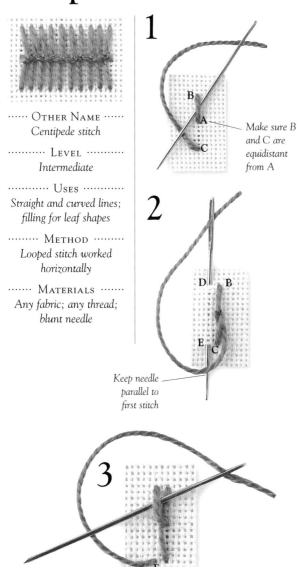

1

Make sure B
and C are
equidistant
from A

2

Keep needle
parallel to
first stitch

3

1 Start at **A**. Make an upright stitch to **B**, then come out directly below **A**, at **C**. Slide the needle under the stitch from right to left, over the working thread.

2 Insert the needle level with **B** at **D**. Come up at **E**, keeping the needle below the working thread.

3 Pass the needle under the previous stitch from right to left, over the working thread. Repeat steps 2 and 3 to continue. Finish off by taking the thread through to the back at the center of the final stitch.

Vandyke

1

2

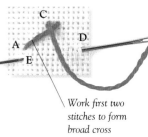

Work first two
stitches to form
broad cross

3

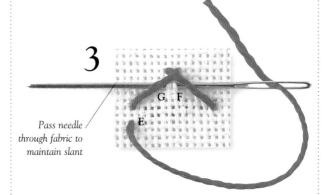

Pass needle
through fabric to
maintain slant

1 Start at **A**. Make a diagonal stitch up to **B** and bring the needle out to the left of **B**, at **C**.

2 Take the needle down and insert level with **A**, at **D**. Come up below **A**, at **E**.

3 Pass the needle under the crossed stitches from **F** to **G**, picking up two threads of background fabric. Repeat steps 2 and 3 to continue.

Ladder

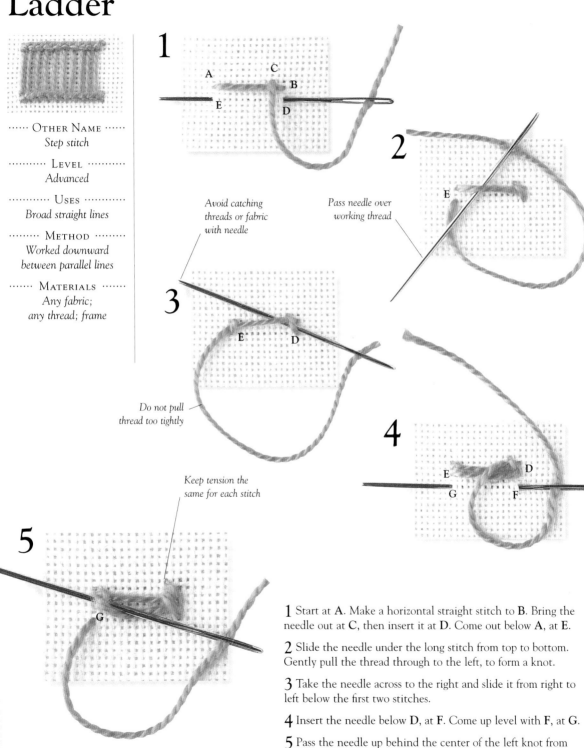

······ OTHER NAME ······
Step stitch

·········· LEVEL ··········
Advanced

··········· USES ···········
Broad straight lines

········ METHOD ········
*Worked downward
between parallel lines*

······ MATERIALS ·······
*Any fabric;
any thread; frame*

*Avoid catching
threads or fabric
with needle*

*Pass needle over
working thread*

*Do not pull
thread too tightly*

*Keep tension the
same for each stitch*

1 Start at **A**. Make a horizontal straight stitch to **B**. Bring the needle out at **C**, then insert it at **D**. Come out below **A**, at **E**.

2 Slide the needle under the long stitch from top to bottom. Gently pull the thread through to the left, to form a knot.

3 Take the needle across to the right and slide it from right to left below the first two stitches.

4 Insert the needle below **D**, at **F**. Come up level with **F**, at **G**.

5 Pass the needle up behind the center of the left knot from right to left. Repeat from step 3 to continue.

Blanket

······ OTHER NAME ······
Open buttonhole stitch

········ LEVEL ········
Easy

······· METHOD ········
*Looped stitch, worked
horizontally*

··········· USES ··········
*Straight or curved borders
and outlines; finishing
edges; securing applique
shapes; filling (see p.87)*

······ MATERIALS ······
*Woven fabrics or felt; any
wool or thread*

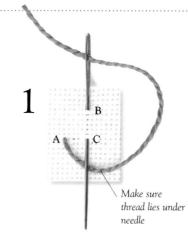

1 *Make sure
thread lies under
needle*

1 Start at **A**. Take the needle up and insert
at **B**, then bring it out directly below and
level with **A**, at **C**.

2 Pull the needle down over the working
thread. Insert the needle at **D** then bring it
out at **E** to make the next stitch. Repeat this
step to continue. Finish off with a tie stitch
(see p.20) over the final loop.

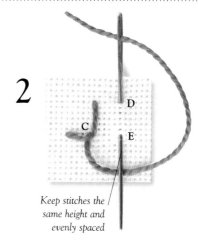

2 *Keep stitches the
same height and
evenly spaced*

········· STITCH VARIATION ·········

Buttonhole stitch is
worked in the same
way but the stitches lie
next to each other to
create a solid line. The background fabric is
completely covered and will not fray, so it is
ideal for cutwork (see pp112-113), and neatening hems and hand-worked buttonholes.

Closed
Buttonhole

········ LEVEL ········
Easy

······· METHOD ········
*Triangular blanket
stitch variation, worked
horizontally*

··········· USES ··········
*Decorative edgings and
borders; in rows as filling*

······ MATERIALS ······
Any fabric; any thread

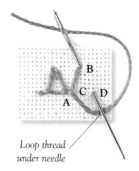

*Loop thread
under needle*

Come up at **A** and insert
the needle at **B**. Bring it up
close to **A**, at **C**. Pull the
needle over the working
thread. Re-insert at **B** and
come up to the right at **D**.
Pull the needle over the
loop. Repeat to continue.

Single Feather

······ OTHER NAME ······
Slanted buttonhole stitch

·········· LEVEL ··········
Easy

······· METHOD ········
*Blanket stitch variation,
worked downward*

··········· USES ··········
*Decorative edging;
outlines and borders;
in smocking; in rows
as open filling*

······ MATERIALS ······
*Any fabric;
any embroidery thread*

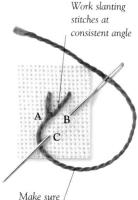

*Work slanting
stitches at
consistent angle*

*Make sure
thread lies
under needle*

Come up at **A**. Take the
needle across to the right
and insert it at **B**. Come out
below **A**, at **C**. Pull the
needle over the working
thread. Repeat to continue.

Up and Down Buttonhole

·········· LEVEL ··········
Intermediate

········ METHOD ········
*Buttonhole stitch
variation, worked
alternately upward
and downward*

··········· USES ···········
*Straight or curved lines
and edgings; in rows
as filling*

······ MATERIALS ······
*Any fabric; any
embroidery thread*

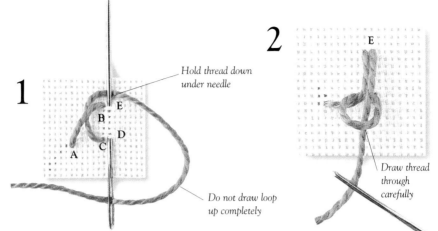

*Hold thread down
under needle*

*Do not draw loop
up completely*

*Draw thread
through
carefully*

1 Start at **A**. Insert the needle at **B** and bring it out at **C**, as for step 1 of blanket stitch (see left). Insert the needle at **D** and bring it out at **E**, making sure the working thread lies under the point. Pull the needle upward, so that the thread forms a loose loop.

2 Take the needle downward, pulling gently until the loop tightens around the base of the two upright stitches. Repeat these two steps to continue.

Open Cretan

·········· LEVEL ··········
Easy

········ METHOD ········
*Looped stitch worked
from top to bottom*

··········· USES ···········
*Curved or straight lines;
open filling*

······ MATERIALS ······
*Any fabric; any thread –
finer threads give a lacy
appearance; frame*

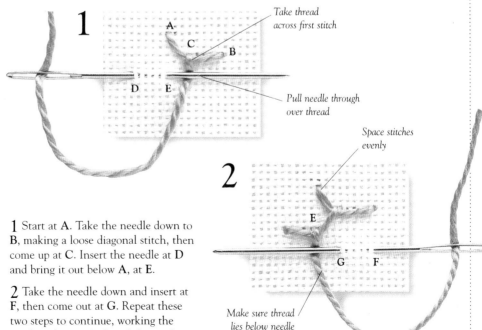

*Take thread
across first stitch*

*Pull needle through
over thread*

*Space stitches
evenly*

*Make sure thread
lies below needle*

1 Start at **A**. Take the needle down to **B**, making a loose diagonal stitch, then come up at **C**. Insert the needle at **D** and bring it out below **A**, at **E**.

2 Take the needle down and insert at **F**, then come out at **G**. Repeat these two steps to continue, working the stitches alternately from left to right.

Feather

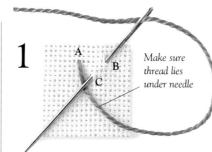

1

Make sure thread lies under needle

2

Do not pull loop too tightly

3

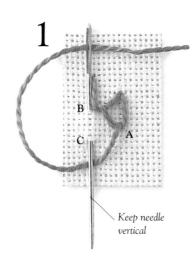

Make all outside stitches point in same direction

····· OTHER NAMES ·····
Briar stitch; single coral stitch

········· LEVEL ·········
Easy

·········· USES ··········
Smocking; hems; crazy patchwork; with ribbon embroidery

········ METHOD ········
Looped stitch, worked alternately from left to right in straight or curved lines

····· MATERIALS ·····
Any fabric; any thread

1 Start at **A** and insert the needle to the right, at **B**, leaving a thread loop. Bring the point out over the thread at **C** and pull through.

2 Insert the needle to the left of **C**, at **D**. Come out directly below **A**, at **E**, and pull through over the loop.

3 Insert the needle at **F** and bring it out at **G**, over the loop. Repeat steps 2 and 3 to continue. Finish off with a tie stitch (see p.20) over the final loop.

Closed Feather

········· LEVEL ·········
Easy

·········· USES ··········
Straight lines and borders; in rows as open filling

········ METHOD ········
Feather variation worked downward

····· MATERIALS ·····
Any fabric; thick threads will give a textured effect

1

Keep needle vertical

2

Make sure upright stitches meet to form solid line

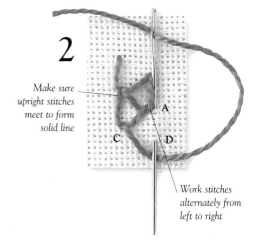

Work stitches alternately from left to right

1 Come up at **A**. Take the needle diagonally up to the left and insert at **B**. Bring the point out over the working thread at **C** and pull through.

2 Re-insert the needle at **A**, bring it out at **D** and pull through over the working thread. Repeat these two steps to continue. Finish off with a tie stitch (see p.20) over the last loop.

Double Feather

····· OTHER NAME ·····
Thorn and briar stitch

········· LEVEL ·········
Easy

·········· USES ··········
*Foliage and branches;
decorating children's
garments*

········ METHOD ········
*Looped stitch,
worked alternately
from left to right*

····· MATERIALS ·····
*Any fabric; fine thread
will give a lacy effect*

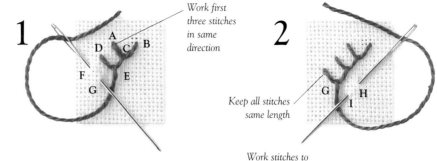

Work first three stitches in same direction

Keep all stitches same length

Work stitches to form a broad zigzag

1 Work the first two stitches as for feather stitch (see p.60), then make a second stitch to the left. Insert the needle level with **E** at **F**, and come out at **G**. Pull the needle through over the loop.

2 Take the needle across to the right and insert at **H**. Come out at **I** and pull through over the loop.

3 Make a second stitch to the right; take the needle down at **J**, bring it out at **K** and pull through over the loop. Continue working downward, making two stitches one side, then the other.

Chained Feather

····· OTHER NAME ·····
Feathered chain stitch

········· LEVEL ·········
Intermediate

·········· USES ··········
*Decorative borders;
foliage*

········ METHOD ········
*Row of slanting picot
stitches set at
alternate angles*

····· MATERIALS ·····
Any fabric; any thread

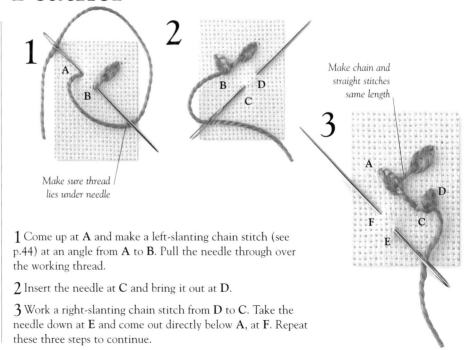

Make sure thread lies under needle

Make chain and straight stitches same length

1 Come up at **A** and make a left-slanting chain stitch (see p.44) at an angle from **A** to **B**. Pull the needle through over the working thread.

2 Insert the needle at **C** and bring it out at **D**.

3 Work a right-slanting chain stitch from **D** to **C**. Take the needle down at **E** and come out directly below **A**, at **F**. Repeat these three steps to continue.

Composite Border Stitches

THIS IS THE most decorative group of stitches which can be worked in single rows, or repeated to create multi-colored fillings with intricate surface textures. Basic outline and border stitches are embellished with interlacing to create some of them, and others are a combination of two or even three stitches. Magic and Singalese chain are flexible stitches which can be sewn along a curved line, but the rest are all made in straight rows. Use a blunt needle for any interlacing,and mount the fabric in an embroidery frame so that the stitches do not become distorted.

Pekinese

····· OTHER NAMES ·····
Chinese stitch;
forbidden stitch

········· LEVEL ·········
Easy

·········· USES ··········
Decorative curved and
straight outlines; in rows
as filling

········ METHOD ········
Laced back stitch, worked
horizontally

····· MATERIALS ·····
Any fabric; lacing can be
worked in thicker thread;
blunt needle

Make loops
same size

Pull needle
over working
thread

Work a row of back stitch (see p.40). Bring the lacing thread out at **A**. Slide the needle upwards beneath **B**, then pass it downwards under **C**. Draw the thread up gently and continue lacing to the end of the row.

Laced Buttonhole

····· OTHER NAME ·····
Threaded buttonhole stitch

········· LEVEL ·········
Easy

·········· USES ··········
Decorative straight
edgings and borders

········ METHOD ········
Two rows of blanket stitch
with interlacing

······· MATERIALS ·······
Any fabric; any thread
in two colors; frame;
blunt needle

Lace under
alternate stitches
at top and bottom

Work two parallel rows of blanket stitch (see p.58) with the upright stitches pointing inward. Bring the lacing thread out at **A**. Slide the needle under **B**, then beneath **C**. Continue lacing to the end of the row.

Interlaced Band

····· OTHER NAMES ·····
Double Pekinese stitch;
herringbone ladder stitch

········· LEVEL ·········
Intermediate

·········· USES ··········
Braided straight lines

········ METHOD ········
Two rows of back stitch
with looped interlacing

····· MATERIALS ·······
Any fabric; any two
threads in the same or
different thicknesses;
frame; blunt needle

1

Use blunt needle
for interlacing

2

Make sure
needle crosses
thread

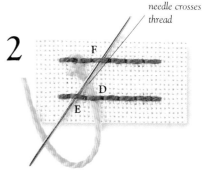

1 Work two parallel lines of back stitch (see p.40), starting the bottom row with a half-length stitch. Bring the lacing thread out at **A**. Pass the needle upwards beneath **B**, then slide it downwards under both **C** and **D**.

2 Take the needle to the left and slide it under **E** and **F**, then pull through. Continue lacing up and down to the end of the row.

········TECHNIQUE VARIATION·········

To create a wider, more open border, work the twisted interlacing over two rows of blanket stitch (see p.58), again using two colors.

Magic Chain

····· OTHER NAMES ·····
*Checkered chain stitch;
two-colored chain stitch*

········· LEVEL ·········
Intermediate

········· USES ·········
Straight or curved outlines

········ METHOD ········
*Chain stitch variation
worked with two threads*

····· MATERIALS ·····
*Any fabric; two
contrasting threads
in the same weight;
long-eyed needle*

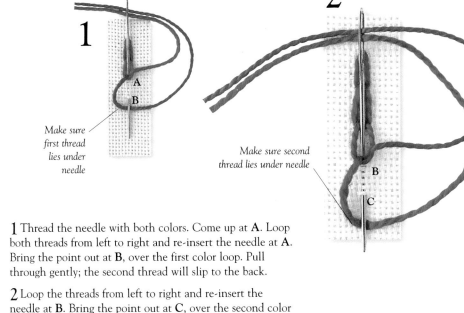

*Make sure
first thread
lies under
needle*

*Make sure second
thread lies under needle*

1 Thread the needle with both colors. Come up at **A**. Loop both threads from left to right and re-insert the needle at **A**. Bring the point out at **B**, over the first color loop. Pull through gently; the second thread will slip to the back.

2 Loop the threads from left to right and re-insert the needle at **B**. Bring the point out at **C**, over the second color loop: pull through. Repeat the steps to the end of the row. Finish with a tie stitch (see p.20) over the last loop.

Singalese Chain

········· LEVEL ·········
Advanced

········· USES ·········
*Decorative borders;
curved or straight
outlines; casing for
narrow ribbon*

········ METHOD ········
*Square chain stitch
worked downward over
contrasting threads*

····· MATERIALS ·····
*Any fabric; any two
different colored threads
of equal weight*

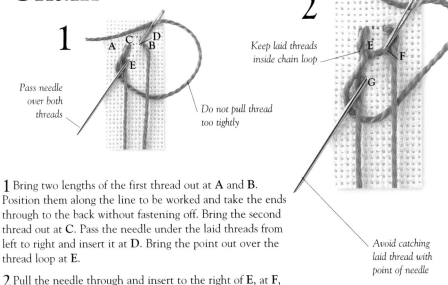

*Pass needle
over both
threads*

*Do not pull thread
too tightly*

*Keep laid threads
inside chain loop*

*Avoid catching
laid thread with
point of needle*

1 Bring two lengths of the first thread out at **A** and **B**. Position them along the line to be worked and take the ends through to the back without fastening off. Bring the second thread out at **C**. Pass the needle under the laid threads from left to right and insert it at **D**. Bring the point out over the thread loop at **E**.

2 Pull the needle through and insert to the right of **E**, at **F**, then bring it out at **G**, ready to work the next stitch. Repeat this step to continue, easing the laid threads into position. Fasten down the final loop with two tie stitches (see p.20) and finish off the laid threads on the reverse side.

Threaded Chain

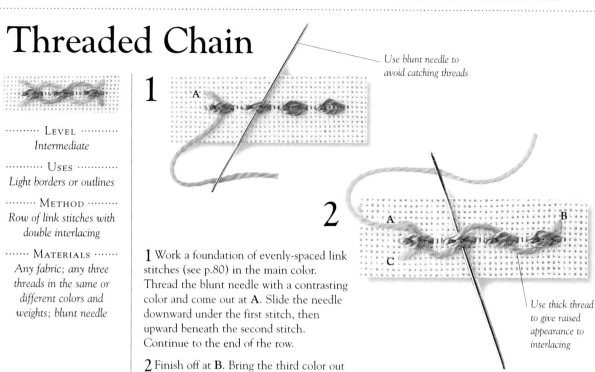

Use blunt needle to avoid catching threads

········ LEVEL ········
Intermediate

········ USES ·········
Light borders or outlines

········ METHOD ········
Row of link stitches with double interlacing

······ MATERIALS ·······
Any fabric; any three threads in the same or different colors and weights; blunt needle

Use thick thread to give raised appearance to interlacing

1 Work a foundation of evenly-spaced link stitches (see p.80) in the main color. Thread the blunt needle with a contrasting color and come out at **A**. Slide the needle downward under the first stitch, then upward beneath the second stitch. Continue to the end of the row.

2 Finish off at **B**. Bring the third color out at **C** and lace it alternately up and down under the link stitches, filling in the spaces.

Guilloche

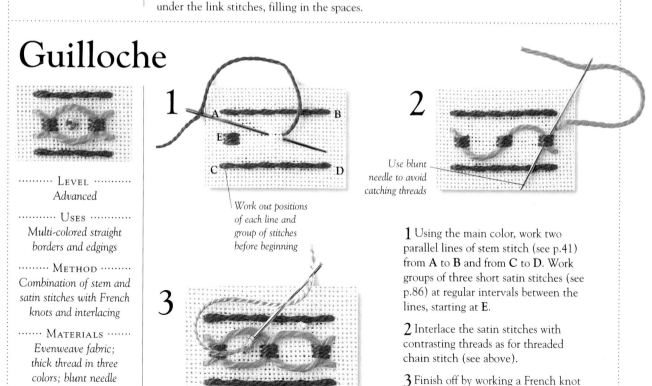

········ LEVEL ········
Advanced

·········· USES ··········
Multi-colored straight borders and edgings

········ METHOD ········
Combination of stem and satin stitches with French knots and interlacing

······ MATERIALS ·······
Evenweave fabric; thick thread in three colors; blunt needle

Work out positions of each line and group of stitches before beginning

Use blunt needle to avoid catching threads

1 Using the main color, work two parallel lines of stem stitch (see p.41) from **A** to **B** and from **C** to **D**. Work groups of three short satin stitches (see p.86) at regular intervals between the lines, starting at **E**.

2 Interlace the satin stitches with contrasting threads as for threaded chain stitch (see above).

3 Finish off by working a French knot (see p.76) in the center of each loop, using the third thread.

Raised Chevron

·········· LEVEL ··········
Intermediate

·········· USES ··········
*Straight outlines
and light borders*

········· METHOD ·········
*Chevron stitch worked
over two lines of
arrowhead stitches*

······ MATERIALS ······
*Any fabric; thicker
thread gives more
texture – choose two
contrasting colors*

*Points of arrowheads
face inward*

*Make sure
stitches are
spaced evenly*

Stitch two parallel rows of
arrowheads (see p.73) in the
first color. Bring the second
thread out at **A** and work a
band of chevron stitch (see
p.49) from left to right, so
that the horizontal stitches
lie across the points of the
arrowhead stitches.

Backstitched Herringbone

·········· LEVEL ··········
Easy

·········· USES ··········
*Open borders; in rows
as lattice filling*

········· METHOD ·········
*Herringbone stitch with
back stitch detail*

······ MATERIALS ······
*Any fabric; two
contrasting threads in the
same or different weights*

*Work back stitches
over crossed threads*

Work a line of herringbone
stitch (see p.52). Using the
second thread, make a back
stitch from **A** to **B**. Bring the
needle up at **C**, insert at **D**,
and come out at **E**. Continue
to the end of the row.

Raised Lattice Band

·········· LEVEL ··········
Advanced

·········· USES ··········
Decorative borders

········· METHOD ·········
*Interlaced herringbone
stitch worked over
padded satin stitch*

······ MATERIALS ······
*Any fabric; lustrous
thread in three colors;
blunt needle; frame*

1

*Work upright
stitches close
together*

2

3

*Make sure lacing is
not pulled too tightly*

1 Work a foundation of long horizontal surface
satin stitch (see p.86). Work a row of upright satin
(see p.86) from left to right over the base stitches.

2 Bring the second thread up at **A** and work a row
of herringbone stitch (see p.52).

3 Thread the blunt needle with the third color
thread. Come up at **A** and slide the needle upward,
under the center of the first long diagonal stitch.
Take it back down under the second stitch from top
to bottom. Continue lacing to the end of the band.

Double Herringbone

····· OTHER NAME ·····
Indian herringbone stitch

········· LEVEL ·········
Advanced

········· USES ·········
*Geometric border; in rows
as open filling*

········ METHOD ········
*Two interlaced rows of
herringbone stitch*

······ MATERIALS ······
*Any fabric; any thick
thread in two colors*

*Slide needle
under previous
stitch*

1

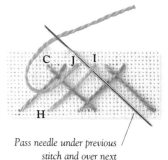

2

*Pass needle under previous
stitch and over next*

3

1 Start at **A** and make a diagonal stitch to **B**.
Bring the needle out at **C**, pass it under the stitch
and take it down at **D**. Come out at **E** and insert at
F. Bring the needle out at **G** and slide it under the
last stitch. Continue to the end of the row.

2 Bring the contrast thread up directly below **C**, at
H. Slide the needle under the second stitch and
insert at **I**. Come out at **J** and pass the needle
under the previous stitch.

3 Insert the needle at **K** and come out at **L**. Take
it over the first thread and under the second.
Repeat steps 2 and 3 to continue.

Twisted Lattice Band

········· LEVEL ·········
Advanced

········· USES ·········
*Ornamental border; in
rows as filling*

········ METHOD ········
*Double herringbone stitch
with two rows of
interlacing*

······ MATERIALS ······
*Any fabric; any thick
thread in two colors*

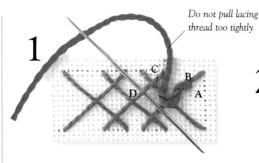

*Do not pull lacing
thread too tightly*

1

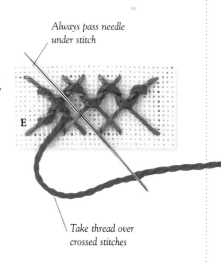

*Always pass needle
under stitch*

2

*Take thread over
crossed stitches*

1 Work a foundation of double herringbone stitch
(see above) in the first color. Bring the lacing thread
out at **A**. Pass the needle downward under **B**, then
upward under **C**. Slide it beneath the next stitch, at
D, from top to bottom.

2 Continue weaving the thread under and over the
top stitches to the end of the row. Bring the thread
out at **E** and interlace the bottom stitches in the
same way to complete.

Butterfly Chain

········· LEVEL ·········
Intermediate

·········· USES ···········
Light frames or borders

········ METHOD ·········
*Twisted chain stitch
worked over groups of
three straight stitches,
without piercing fabric*

······ MATERIALS ·······
*Any fabric; thick thread in
two colors; blunt needle*

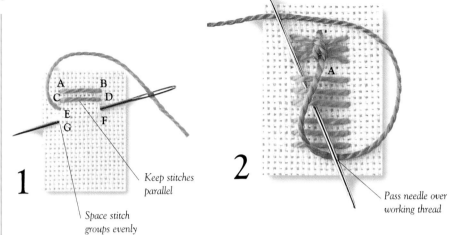

1 *Keep stitches
parallel*

*Space stitch
groups evenly*

1 Start at **A**, and make a horizontal stitch across to **B**. Work two more stitches directly below, from **C** to **D** and **E** to **F**, then bring the needle out at **G** to work the next group of three stitches.

2 *Pass needle over
working thread*

2 Using the contrast thread, work a twisted chain stitch (see p.44) over each group of horizontal stitches. Come through at **A** and loop the thread to the right. Slide the needle under all three stitches and pull it through. Tighten the thread to draw the stitches together.

Raised Chain Band

···· OTHER NAME ·····
Raised chain stitch

·········· LEVEL ··········
Intermediate

·········· USES ··········
Heavy borders

········ METHOD ·········
*Chain stitch worked over
straight stitch foundation,
without piercing fabric*

······ MATERIALS ·······
*Any fabric; any thick
thread in two colors;
blunt needle*

*Keep needle to
left of working
thread*

2

*Do not space stitches
too far apart*

1

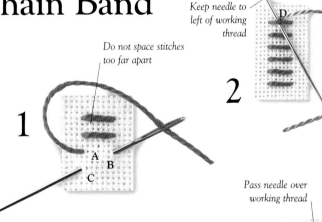

*Pass needle over
working thread*

3

*Do not pull
thread up
too tightly*

1 Work a stack of short parallel stitches. Bring the needle out at **A** and take it down at **B**. Come up at **C** and continue working downward.

2 Bring the second thread out at **D**. Pass the needle under the first stitch from bottom to top.

3 Loop the thread to the right. Slide the needle downward under the first stitch, to the right of **D**. Repeat steps 2 and 3 to the end of the stack.

Diagonal Woven Band

·········· LEVEL ··········
Advanced

·········· USES ··········
*Dense striped border
or frame*

········· METHOD ·········
*Two contrasting threads
woven through row of
straight stitches*

······ MATERIALS ······
*Any fabric; any
two twisted threads;
two blunt needles*

1

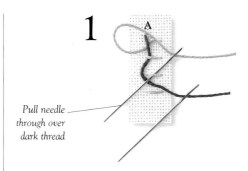

A

*Pull needle
through over
dark thread*

1 Work a stack of straight stitches (see p.68, raised chain band step 1). Bring the dark thread up at **A**, pass the needle under the second stitch and take it to the right. Bring the light thread up at **A**. Slide the needle to the left below the first stitch and the dark thread, then take it under the third stitch and across the dark thread.

2 Continue weaving downward, taking the two threads alternately under and over the straight stitches. Work the following rows in the same way, alternating the color of the first stitch.

*Work with
long threads to
avoid joins*

2

········ STITCH VARIATION ········

To work striped woven band stitch, start every twisted line with the same color thread, to create solid blocks of alternate colors.

Portuguese Border

·········· LEVEL ··········
Advanced

·········· USES ··········
Raised borders

········· METHOD ·········
*Diagonal stitches woven
over straight stitch
foundation*

······ MATERIALS ······
*Any fabric; twisted
thread in two colors;
blunt needle*

1

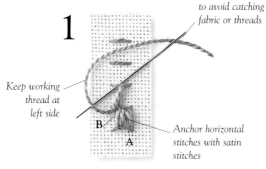

*Use blunt needle
to avoid catching
fabric or threads*

*Keep working
thread at
left side*

B

A

*Anchor horizontal
stitches with satin
stitches*

1 Work a stack of horizontal stitches (see p.68, raised chain band step 1). Bring the second thread up at **A** and make three satin stitches (see p.86) over the first two stitches. Come out at **B** and slide the needle downward under the next two horizontal stitches, making a slanting stitch. Pass the needle under the third horizontal stitch again, to make a second stitch. Continue upward, working pairs of slanting stitches.

2 At the top of the stack, take the needle down at **C** and out at **D**. Pass it upward under the top two stitches. Continue as before, slanting the stitches in the opposite direction.

2

C D

B

*Keep thread to
right of stitches*

FILLING
STITCHES

POWDERED FILLING AND
ISOLATED STITCHES

· · · · · · · ◆ · · · · · · ·

OPEN AND SOLID
FILLING STITCHES

Powdered Filling and Isolated Stitches

THESE DETACHED STITCHES are all worked singly and vary considerably in size. The larger versions are often used as accent stitches, while the smaller ones are repeated to form a powdered filling. The stitches can be arranged in several ways: in regular rows to form straight lines and geometric patterns; scattered randomly; spaced apart to allow the background fabric to show through, or sewn close together to form a dense, textured surface. A design usually requires a powdered filling to be contained within an area which has been defined with an outline or border stitch.

Straight

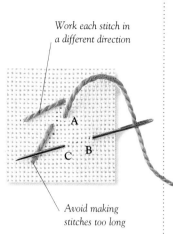

Work each stitch in a different direction

Avoid making stitches too long

····· OTHER NAME ·····
Stroke stitch

········· LEVEL ·········
Easy

··········· USES ···········
Foliage; textured filling

········· METHOD ·········
Randomly placed single stitches of varying length

······ MATERIALS ······
Any fabric; any thread

Come up at **A**. Take the needle down to **B** and insert, then bring it out at **C**. Continue working straight stitches in a random pattern to fill the required area.

Arrowhead

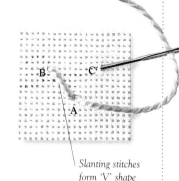

Slanting stitches form 'V' shape

········· LEVEL ·········
Easy

··········· USES ···········
Powdered filling; worked in vertical or horizontal rows as border stitch

········· METHOD ·········
Two straight stitches worked at a right angle

······ MATERIALS ······
Any fabric; thick threads create raised effect

Start at **A**. Make a diagonal straight stitch up to **B**, then come out again at **A**. Insert the needle at **C** to complete.

Seeding

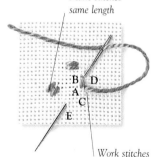

Make stitches same length

Work stitches in different directions

····· OTHER NAME ·····
Backstitched seeding

········· LEVEL ·········
Easy

··········· USES ···········
Powdered filling; worked in rows as outline

········· METHOD ·········
Pairs of short, closely spaced back stitches

······ MATERIALS ······
Any fabric; pearl thread makes stitches stand out

Come up at **A**. Insert the needle at **B** and bring it out at **C**. Insert at **D** to complete the second stitch, then bring the needle up at **E** to work the next pair of stitches.

St George Cross

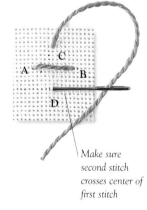

Make sure second stitch crosses center of first stitch

····· OTHER NAME ·····
Upright cross stitch

········· LEVEL ·········
Easy

··········· USES ···········
Geometric or random fillings; isolated stitch

······ MATERIALS ······
Any fabric; twisted threads give raised effect

Start at **A** and work a horizontal straight stitch across to **B**. Come out at **C**. Take the needle down over the first stitch and insert at **D** to complete the cross.

Ermine

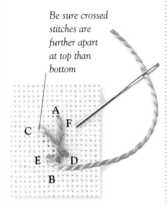

Be sure crossed stitches are further apart at top than bottom

······ LEVEL ······
Easy

········ USES ········
Scattered or regular filling; in rows as border; isolated stitch; in blackwork

······ METHOD ······
Wide cross stitch worked over upright straight stitch

····· MATERIALS ·····
Evenweave fabric for a regular effect; any thread

Start at **A** and work a vertical straight stitch to **B**. Bring the needle out at **C** and insert at **D**. Come out at **E**. Take the needle across the two stitches and insert at **F** to complete.

Square Boss

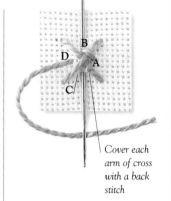

Cover each arm of cross with a back stitch

····· OTHER NAME ·····
Raised knot

······ LEVEL ······
Intermediate

········ USES ········
Light fillings; in rows as border; isolated stitch

······ METHOD ······
Cross stitch covered by back stitch square

····· MATERIALS ·····
Any fabric; thick thread gives raised texture

Make a cross stitch (see p.50). Bring the needle out at **A** and take it down at **B**. Come out at **C** and insert at **A**. Bring the needle out at **D** and insert at **C**. Work a back stitch from **B** to **D** to complete.

Star

······ LEVEL ······
Intermediate

········ USES ········
Scattered as light filling; in rows as border; isolated stitch

······ METHOD ······
Elongated cross stitch worked over St George cross and cross stitches

····· MATERIALS ·····
Any fabric; any thread

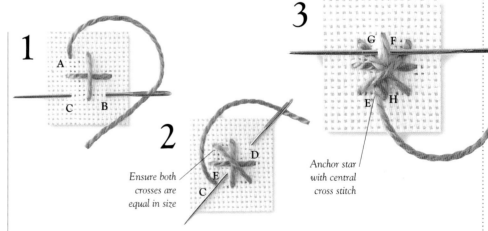

Ensure both crosses are equal in size

Anchor star with central cross stitch

1 Make a St George cross stitch (see p.73). Bring the needle out at **A**, and work a diagonal stitch down to **B**. Come out to the left of **B**, at **C**.

2 Take the needle diagonally up to **D** and insert. Come out near the center of the stitch at **E**.

3 Insert the needle at **F**, then bring it out to the left at **G**. Take it down at **H** to complete the cross.

······ TECHNIQUE VARIATION ······

For a decorative effect, stitch the small cross in the center of the star (see step 3) using a different colored thread.

Woven Star

.... LEVEL ....
Intermediate

.... USES ....
Powdered filling;
isolated stitch

.... METHOD ....
Five interwoven
straight stitches

.... MATERIALS ....
Any fabric; any thread

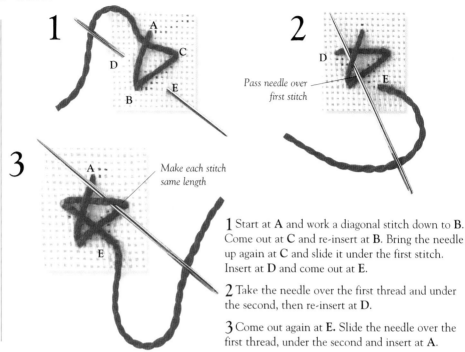

Pass needle over
first stitch

Make each stitch
same length

1 Start at **A** and work a diagonal stitch down to **B**. Come out at **C** and re-insert at **B**. Bring the needle up again at **C** and slide it under the first stitch. Insert at **D** and come out at **E**.

2 Take the needle over the first thread and under the second, then re-insert at **D**.

3 Come out again at **E**. Slide the needle over the first thread, under the second and insert at **A**.

Woven Cross

.... LEVEL ....
Intermediate

.... USES ....
Powdered filling;
isolated stitch

.... METHOD ....
Four interwoven
straight stitches

.... MATERIALS ....
Any fabric;
any thick thread

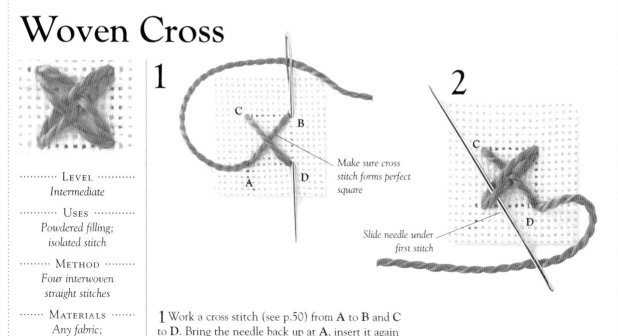

Make sure cross
stitch forms perfect
square

Slide needle under
first stitch

1 Work a cross stitch (see p.50) from **A** to **B** and **C** to **D**. Bring the needle back up at **A**, insert it again at **B** and come out at **D**.

2 Pass the needle under the first thread and over the second, then insert at **C** to complete the cross.

French Knot

Hold thread to keep it taut

Take needle down at point where it emerged

········· LEVEL ·········
Intermediate

········· USES ·········
Light or solid powdered filling; singly as raised highlight

········· METHOD ·········
Twisted knotted stitch

····· MATERIALS ·····
Any fabric; any thread depending on size; small-eyed needle

1 Start at **A**. Hold the thread taut and wrap it twice around the needle, then pull it gently to tighten the loops.

2 Maintaining the tension, insert the needle again at **A**, pushing it down through the two loops to form a round knot.

········· STITCH VARIATION ·········

To work pistil stitch, insert the needle a short distance from where it emerged, to form a long tail. Make eight stitches in a circle to create a flower center or floral shape.

Bullion Knot

Hold coiled thread in place as needle is pulled through

Pull thread up gently

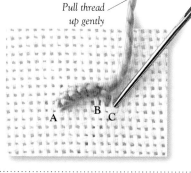

····· OTHER NAME ·····
Caterpillar stitch

········· LEVEL ·········
Intermediate

········· USES ·········
Powdered filling; accent stitch; in rows as border

········· METHOD ·········
Long twisted knot

····· MATERIALS ·····
Any fabric; any twisted embroidery thread

1 Start at **A**. Take the needle down at **B** and bring the point back through at **A**.

2 Wrap the thread six times around the needle, holding the loops down with a finger. Using the other hand, pull the needle carefully through the fabric and the coiled thread.

3 Take the needle back down at **C** and pull the working thread up so that the loops lie flat.

Danish Knot

········· LEVEL ·········
Intermediate

··········· USES ···········
*Powdered filling;
triangular accent stitch*

········· METHOD ·········
*Looped knot worked over
short diagonal stitch*

········ MATERIALS ········
*Any fabric;
thick twisted thread*

1

*Pull loop up
gently to form
first part of
knot*

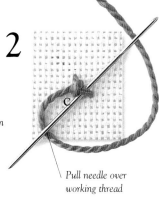

2

*Pull needle over
working thread*

3

1 Start at **A** and work a short diagonal stitch down to **B**. Bring the needle out at **C** and slide it under the stitch from right to left.

2 Take the needle across to the right of the knot. Pass it under the diagonal stitch from right to left for a second time.

3 Insert the needle at **C** to complete the knot.

Four-legged Knot

····· OTHER NAME ·····
Knot stitch

·········· LEVEL ··········
Intermediate

··········· USES ···········
*Powdered filling;
isolated stitch*

········ METHOD ········
*Upright cross with
knotted center*

······ MATERIALS ······
Any fabric; any thick thread

1

2

1 Start at **A** and work an upright stitch down to **B**. Come out at **C**. Loop the thread to the left, and slide the needle under the stitch.

2 Pull the thread gently to form a knot. Insert the needle at **D** to complete the stitch.

Sword

·········· LEVEL ··········
Easy

··········· USES ···········
*Worked randomly as light
filling; in rows as border*

········· METHOD ·········
Looped, elongated cross

······ MATERIALS ······
*Any fabric; any
thick thread*

*Make sure B is
equidistant
from A and C*

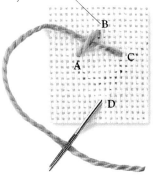

Start at **A** and work a loose diagonal stitch up to **B**. Bring the needle out at **C** and slide it under the stitch from right to left. Take it down at **D**, pulling gently so that the two stitches form a cross.

Fly

····· OTHER NAMES ·····
Y-stitch; open loop stitch

········· LEVEL ·········
Easy

········· USES ·········
*Light or heavy filling;
worked in horizontal or
vertical rows as border*

········ METHOD ········
Tied loop stitch

····· MATERIALS ·····
*Any fabric;
any thick thread*

1

*Pull needle over
working thread*

2

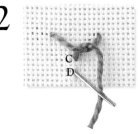

1 Start at **A** and work a loose horizontal stitch across to **B**. Bring the needle out at **C**.

2 Take the needle down at **D** to make a tie stitch (see p.20).

Sheaf Filling

········· LEVEL ·········
Intermediate

········· USES ·········
*Powdered filling; in rows
as border; isolated stitch*

········ METHOD ········
*Three upright straight
stitches tied at the center*

····· MATERIALS ·····
*Any fabric; any thick
thread*

*Pull stitches together to
create sheaf effect*

Make three parallel straight stitches from **A** to **B**, **C** to **D** and **E** to **F**. Come up at **G** and pass the needle to the left, under the first stitch. Take the needle across to the right and slide it back under the stitches. Take it to the right again and pull the thread up gently. Insert at **G** to complete.

Crown

········· LEVEL ·········
Intermediate

········· USES ·········
*Powdered filling; in rows
as border; isolated stitch*

········ METHOD ········
*Looped stitch tied down
with three straight stitches*

····· MATERIALS ·····
*Any fabric; any thick
thread*

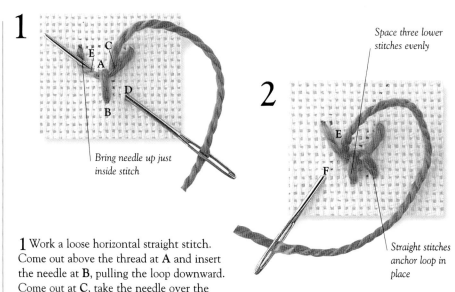

1

*Bring needle up just
inside stitch*

2

*Space three lower
stitches evenly*

*Straight stitches
anchor loop in
place*

1 Work a loose horizontal straight stitch. Come out above the thread at **A** and insert the needle at **B**, pulling the loop downward. Come out at **C**, take the needle over the thread and insert at **D**, then come out at **E**.

2 Take the needle down over the thread and insert at **F** to complete the stitch.

Sorbello

········· LEVEL ·········
Intermediate

··········· USES ···········
*In straight rows as filling;
in rows as border;
isolated stitch*

········· METHOD ·········
Heavy square knot

······· MATERIALS ·······
*Any fabric; twisted or
pearl threads give a
raised effect*

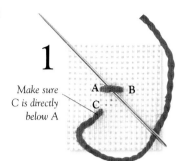

1
*Make sure
C is directly
below A*

A   B
C

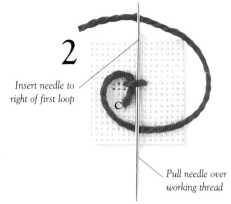

2
*Insert needle to
right of first loop*

C

*Pull needle over
working thread*

1 Start at **A** and work a short stitch to **B**.
Bring the needle out below **A**, at **C**, and
slide it under the stitch from bottom to top.

2 Hold the thread down to the left and
pass the needle under the stitch again, this
time from top to bottom.

3 Pull the thread gently to make a knot,
then insert the needle below **B** at **D** to
complete the stitch.

3

B
C   D

Palestrina Knot

········· LEVEL ·········
Intermediate

··········· USES ···········
*Geometric filling;
worked in rows as border;
isolated stitch*

········· METHOD ·········
Rectangular looped knot

······· MATERIALS ·······
*Any fabric;
any thick thread*

1
B
A   C

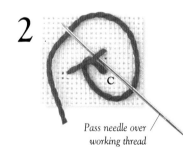

2
C

*Pass needle over
working thread*

1 Start at **A** and work a diagonal stitch to
B. Bring the needle out level with **A**, at **C**,
and slide it under the stitch from
top to bottom.

2 Pass the needle under the diagonal
stitch again, from top to bottom and to the
right of the first loop.

3 Pull the thread gently to form a knot,
then take the needle down diagonally
opposite **C**, at **D**, to complete the stitch.

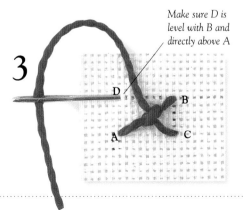

*Make sure D is
level with B and
directly above A*

3
D   B
A   C

Link

···· OTHER NAME ····
Detached chain stitch

········ LEVEL ·········
Easy

··········· USES ···········
*Scattered as light filling;
leaves and flower petals*

········ METHOD ········
Single looped stitch

········ MATERIALS ········
Any fabric; any thread

*Hold thread down
to side of needle*

1 Start at **A**. Make a loop and take the needle down at **A**. Come out at **B** and pull the needle through over the working thread.

2 Insert the needle directly below **B**, at **C**, making a tie stitch (see p.20) to complete.

*Tie stitch
secures loop*

········ STITCH VARIATION ········

Lazy daisy stitch is formed by making several link stitches in a circle, all starting at the center. Each stitch represents a petal and the whole looks like a flowerhead.

Berry

········ LEVEL ·········
Intermediate

··········· USES ···········
*Powdered filling;
flowers and leaves*

········ METHOD ········
Double link stitch

········ MATERIALS ········
Any fabric; any thread

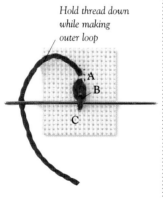

*Hold thread down
while making
outer loop*

Make a small link stitch (see above). Bring the needle out at **A** and slide it under the tie stitch between **B** and **C**. Take the needle back up and insert at **A** to complete the stitch.

Long-tailed Daisy

···· OTHER NAME ····
Picot stitch

········ LEVEL ·········
Easy

··········· USES ···········
*Powdered filling; in circles
as floral motif*

········ METHOD ········
*Link variation with
long tie stitch*

········ MATERIALS ········
Any fabric; any thread

*Work elongated
tie stitch to
form tail*

Start at **A** and follow step 1 of link stitch (see above). Take the needle down below **B**, at **C**, to make a long tie stitch.

Detached Wheatear

1 *Make sure C is equidistant from A and B*

2 *Bring needle out directly below C*

3

······ OTHER NAMES ······
Tete-de-boeuf stitch;
ox-head stitch

········· LEVEL ·········
Intermediate

··········· USES ···········
Powdered filling;
isolated stitch

········ METHOD ········
Link stitch worked over
loose straight stitch

······· MATERIALS ·······
Any fabric; any thread

1 Start at **A**. Insert the needle at **B** and bring it out at **C**, passing over the working thread.

2 Make a loop and take the needle down at **C**. Come out at **D**, passing the needle over the working thread.

3 Take the needle down at **E** to form a short tie stitch (see p.20) to complete.

Tulip

1

2 *Make sure E is level with D*

········· LEVEL ·········
Intermediate

··········· USES ···········
In alternate rows as
powdered filling;
naturalistic flowers

········ METHOD ········
Straight stitch worked
through link stitch

······· MATERIALS ·······
Any fabric; any thread

1 Start at **A** and work a long-tailed daisy stitch (see p.80). Take the needle down at **C** and bring it out to the left, at **D**.

2 Pass the needle under the tie stitch and insert it at **E** to complete the 'leaves'.

······· TECHNIQUE VARIATION ·······
Make a slanting straight stitch on either side of the picot stitch instead of a single one passing beneath the tie stitch (see step 2 above). This creates the effect of two separate leaves at the base of the flower.

Woven Spider Web

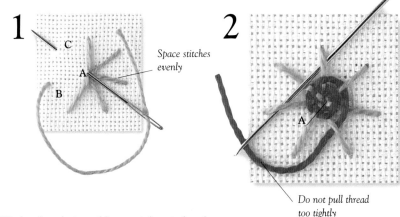

1 *Space stitches evenly*

C
A
B

2 *Do not pull thread too tightly*

A

········ LEVEL ········
Intermediate

········· USES ·········
Isolated stitch; large-scale powdered filling

········ METHOD ········
Solid circle woven on foundation of seven straight stitches

······· MATERIALS ·······
Any fabric; any thread in two colors; blunt needle

1 Work a foundation of five straight stitches (see p.73), all radiating from **A**. Bring the needle up at **B** and take it back down at **A**. Come out at **C**, ready to work the final stitch.

2 Bring the second thread up at **A**. Working clockwise, weave it alternately over and under the straight stitches until only the tips are left uncovered. Take the needle to the back to finish.

············ STITCH VARIATION ············
To make a ribbon rose, use a length of narrow silk embroidery ribbon for the weaving in step 2 (see above). Allow it to twist slightly to create the raised petal effect.

Ribbed Web

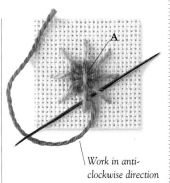

A

Work in anti-clockwise direction

···· OTHER NAME ····
Ribbed spider web

········ LEVEL ········
Intermediate

········· USES ·········
Isolated stitch

········ METHOD ········
Back stitched spiral over large star stitch

······· MATERIALS ·······
Any fabric; any thick thread in two colors; blunt needle

Work a star stitch (see p.74) omitting the final cross. Come up at **A**. Slide the needle under the first two stitches to the left, then take it under the second and third stitches, making a back stitch (see p.40). Continue working round the star stitch until only the tips can be seen.

Buttonhole Wheel

Space stitches evenly around outer circle

A
B
C

········ LEVEL ········
Intermediate

········· USES ·········
Isolated stitch

········ METHOD ········
Buttonhole stitch worked within a ring

······· MATERIALS ·······
Any fabric; any thread

Mark two concentric circles. Come up at **A**, and insert the needle at **B** on the inner circle. Bring the needle out at **C**, passing it over the working thread. Continue stitching until the ring is complete.

Shisha

·········· LEVEL ··········
Advanced

·········· USES ··········
*Indian embroidery; with
couched gold threads*

·········· METHOD ··········
*Mirror disc attached
to fabric with ring of
twisted stitches*

·········· MATERIALS ·······
*Any fabric; any thick
thread; shisha mirror;
frame*

1

*Make four
straight stitches
to anchor mirror*

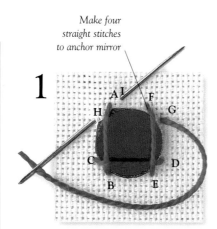

2

*Work diagonal
stitches over
straight stitches*

3

*Pass needle over
working thread*

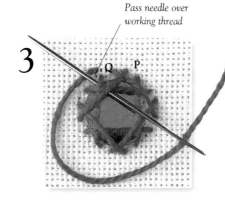

4

*Make sure thread
lies under needle*

5

*Keep tension even when
working twisted stitches*

1 Place the mirror in position. Start at **A** and work a straight stitch down to **B**. Come out at **C** and insert at **D**. Come up at **E** and down at **F**, then come out at **G** and go down at **H**. Bring the needle up at **I**, ready to start the next four stitches.

2 Take the needle down to **J** to make a diagonal stitch. Bring it out at **K** and insert at **L**. Come out at **M**, down at **N**, out at **O**, then take the needle up to **P** and insert.

3 Bring the needle out at **Q**, just outside the straight stitches and pass it beneath the threads from right to left.

4 Insert the needle at **R** and bring it up at **S**, to make a small back stitch. Pull it through over the working thread.

5 Slide the needle back under the straight stitches and pull it through gently over the looped thread. Repeat steps **4** and **5** all the way around the mirror to complete.

Open and Solid Filling Stitches

B OTH TYPES OF filling are stitched within a marked outline, which may be a curved naturalistic shape or a geometric block. Open fillings allow the background to show through, whereas solid fillings produce a densely stitched area and should be worked in a thick thread that covers the fabric completely. Some of these stitches have evolved as shading stitches, using several closely toning threads. With practise, these can produce subtle, three-dimensional effects, especially for flowers and foliage. The fabric should be mounted in a frame for all filling stitches.

Damask Darning

c B A

Work stitches so that spaces between them create a pattern

······ OTHER NAME ······
Damask stitch

········ LEVEL ········
Easy

······ USES ······
Solid filling patterns; geometric bands

······ METHOD ······
Closely spaced rows of running stitch

······ MATERIALS ······
Evenweave fabric; any thread

Come up at **A**, to the right of the start of the stitch above. Insert the needle at **B**, to the right of the end of the stitch above. Bring the needle up one thread to the left, at **C**. Repeat, always following the previous line of stitching.

Double Darning

Work stitches to form vertical ridges

F E D C B   A

Be sure each row of stitches lines up with previous one

········ LEVEL ········
Intermediate

········ USES ········
Solid filling stitch that appears the same at front and back

········ METHOD ········
Double running stitch in closely spaced rows

········ MATERIALS ········
Evenweave fabric; any thread

Work a row of evenly spaced running stitches (see p.39), from **A** to **B**, **C** to **D** and **E** to **F**. Fill in the spaces on the return journey; bring the needle back out at **E**, insert at **D** and come out at **C**. Work the following rows directly above.

Brick and Cross Filling

1

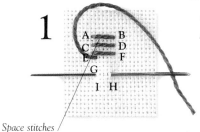

A   B
C   D
E   F
G
I H

Space stitches equally

2

E   J
L
K

K lies directly below E

········ LEVEL ········
Intermediate

········ USES ········
Open geometric filling

········ METHOD ········
Alternate cross and groups of straight stitches, worked in vertical rows

······ MATERIALS ······
Evenweave fabric; any thread

1 Make three parallel straight stitches from **A** to **B**, **C** to **D** and **E** to **F**. Bring the needle out at **G**. Work a diagonal stitch to **H**, then come out directly below **G**, at **I**.

2 Insert the needle at **J** to complete the cross stitch. Bring the needle out to the left of **I**, at **K**.

3 Insert at **L**, then make two more straight stitches. Come out level with **L**, at **M**, and insert at **N**. Bring the needle out at **O** and insert it at **P** to complete the second cross stitch. Come out at **Q** to begin the next three straight stitches.

3

Be sure top diagonal stitches lie in same direction

K   Q   L
M   P
O   N

Satin

····· OTHER NAME ·····
Damask stitch

········· LEVEL ·········
Intermediate

·········· USES ··········
Solid filling; bands

········ METHOD ········
Closely worked straight stitches

······· MATERIALS ·······
*Any fabric; any thread –
stranded silk or cotton
gives lustrous finish*

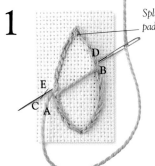

1

*Split stitch creates
padded edge*

2

*Leave no space
between stitches*

*Work each stitch
at same angle*

1 Outline the area to be covered with split stitch (see p.40). Start the satin stitch at the widest point of the shape. Work a diagonal stitch from **A** up to **B** and bring the needle out next to **A**, at **C**. Take it down next to **B**, at **D**. Come out at **E** ready for the next stitch.

2 Repeat, varying the stitch length until the top part of the shape is covered. Bring the needle out again just below **A** and work downward to fill the rest of the shape.

······· TECHNIQUE VARIATION ·······

When working satin stitch over a geometric shape or as a border, work the stitches at a right angle to the outline. Start stitching at one end and work to the other.

Surface Satin

········· LEVEL ·········
Intermediate

·········· USES ··········
Solid filling; bands

········ METHOD ········
Closely worked straight stitches: uses less thread than satin stitch

······· MATERIALS ·······
*Any fabric; any thread –
stranded silk or cotton for
smooth surface; frame*

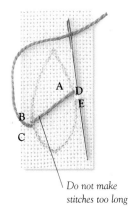

*Do not make
stitches too long*

Mark the required shape. Work a diagonal stitch from **A** down to **B** and come up directly below, at **C**. Take the needle up to **D** and bring it out at **E**. Fill the lower part of the shape in this way. Come back up above **A** to work the remaining area.

Encroaching Satin

········· LEVEL ·········
Intermediate

·········· USES ··········
*Solid filling for
larger areas*

········ METHOD ········
*Overlapping narrow
rows of satin stitch*

······· MATERIALS ·······
*Any fabric; any thread,
in shades of the same
color; frame*

*Insert needle
just above base
of previous
stitches*

Work a row of satin stitch (see above). On the following rows, bring the needle out at **A** and insert at **B**, between two stitches on the row above. Come up next to **A**, at **C**. Repeat to the row's end.

Long and Short

········ LEVEL ··········
Advanced

·········· USES ············
*Shaded filling, giving
three-dimensional effect*

········ METHOD ········
Interlocking satin stitches

······ MATERIALS ·······
*Any fabric; any thread,
in shades of the same
color; frame*

1

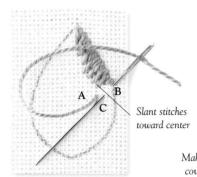

Slant stitches
toward center

2

*Make stitches all
same length*

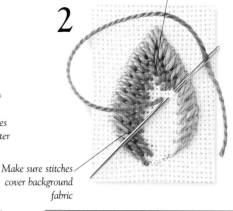

*Make sure stitches
cover background
fabric*

1 Mark the outline of the area to be stitched.
Work a row of alternate long and short satin
stitches (see p.86) around the edge. Come up at
A and take the needle down at **B** to make a long
stitch. Bring it out at **C** to make a short stitch.
Continue in this way to complete the first round.

2 Using a darker shade, work a row of long satin
stitches which interlock with the first round. Fill
in the center with a third shade.

·········· TECHNIQUE VARIATION···········

When filling square or
rectangular shapes, work
the first row in alternate
long and short stitches
and subsequent rows in
long stitches only, so
they interlock as before.

Buttonhole Filling

···· OTHER NAME ·····
Buttonhole shading

········· LEVEL ··········
Intermediate

············ USES ············
Shaded filling

······· METHOD ········
*Overlapping rows of
buttonhole stitch*

······ MATERIALS ·······
*Any fabric; any thread,
in shades of the same
color; frame*

Work a row of buttonhole
stitch (see p.58) using the
lightest thread. With a darker
tone, work the second row
directly below, so that the
upright stitches overlap the
base of the previous row.
Work subsequent rows in
progressively darker tones to
create the effect of shading.

Stem Filling

····· OTHER NAME ·····
Stem stitch shading

·········· LEVEL ··········
Intermediate

············ USES ············
Shaded filling

········· METHOD ········
*Closely spaced lines of
stem stitch*

······· MATERIALS ·······
*Any fabric; any thread, in
shades of the same color*

Mark the outline of the area
to be stitched. Using the
darkest thread, work two rows
of stem stitch (see p.41) along
one side of the outline. Work
the next two rows in a lighter
shade. Continue to fill the
shape with rows of stem
stitch, graduating the color to
create a shaded effect.

Leaf

·········· LEVEL ··········
Intermediate

·········· USES ··········
*Open filling for leaves,
petals and wide borders*

········ METHOD ········
*Overlapping diagonal
stitches worked upward*

······ MATERIALS ······
*Any fabric;
any thread; frame*

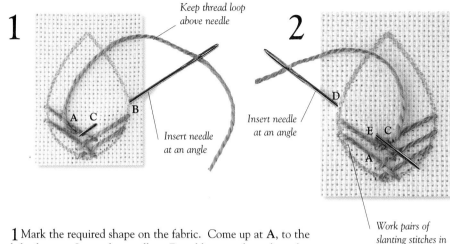

*Keep thread loop
above needle*

*Insert needle
at an angle*

*Insert needle
at an angle*

*Work pairs of
slanting stitches in
alternate directions*

1 Mark the required shape on the fabric. Come up at **A**, to the left of center. Insert the needle at **B** and bring it through to the right of center, at **C**.

2 Take the needle down at **D** and bring it up directly above **A**, at **E**. Repeat these two stitches to fill the space, decreasing the length as the leaf tapers to a point. Work a narrow outline stitch (see pp.38–46) around the outside edge to complete.

Open Fishbone

·········· LEVEL ··········
Easy

·········· USES ··········
*Light filling for small leaf or
petal shapes; open borders*

········ METHOD ········
*Alternate slanting stitches,
worked downward*

······ MATERIALS ······
*Any fabric; any thread;
frame*

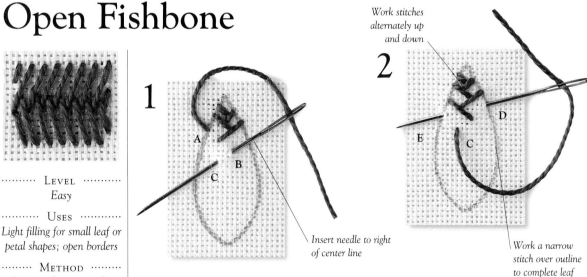

*Work stitches
alternately up
and down*

*Insert needle to right
of center line*

*Work a narrow
stitch over outline
to complete leaf*

1 Mark the required shape. Come up at **A** and make a downward slanting stitch to **B**, to the right of center. Bring the needle out to the left of center, at **C**.

2 Take the needle up to the right and insert at **D**. Come out at **E**, ready to work the next downward stitch. Repeat these two stitches to continue, altering the length as the outline widens or narrows.

Attached Fly

····· OTHER NAME ·····
Fishbone

········· LEVEL ·········
Easy

·········· USES ··········
*Open filling for narrow
leaf or geometric shapes;
light borders*

········ METHOD ········
*Row of linked fly stitches
worked downward*

····· MATERIALS ·····
*Any fabric; any thread;
embroidery frame*

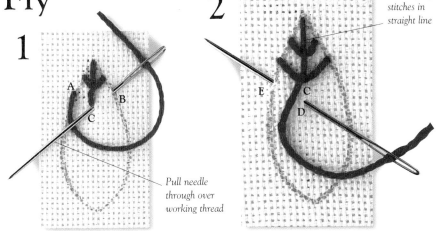

1
*Pull needle
through over
working thread*

2
*Work upright
stitches in
straight line*

1 Mark the outline of the area to be filled.
Come out at **A** and insert the needle on the
same level, at **B**. Bring it up in the center at **C**.

2 Insert the needle directly below **C**, at **D**, to
make a straight stitch, and bring it out at **E**.
Repeat steps 1 and 2 to continue, varying the
stitch length as required.

········· STITCH VARIATION ·········

Close fly stitch is
made by reducing
the length of the
straight stitches
(see step 2).

Cretan

····· OTHER NAME ·····
Cretan filling

········· LEVEL ·········
Easy

·········· USES ··········
*Open filling for leaf or
geometric motif; borders*

········ METHOD ········
*Looped vertical stitch,
worked downward*

····· MATERIALS ·····
*Any fabric;
any thread; frame*

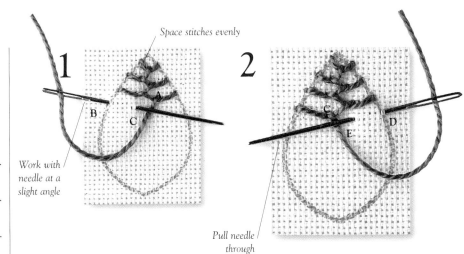

1
Space stitches evenly

*Work with
needle at a
slight angle*

2

*Pull needle
through
over loop*

1 Mark the shape to be filled. Come up to the
right of center at **A**, then take the needle across to
B and insert. Come out to the left of center at **C**.
Pull the needle through over the working thread.

2 Take the needle down at **D** and come out at **E**.
Repeat these two steps to fill the required area.

········· STITCH VARIATION ·········

Close Cretan stitch
is formed by working
each new stitch
immediately below

the last, so no space is left between them.

Romanian Couching

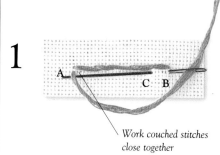

Work couched stitches close together

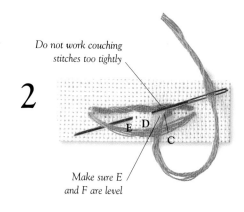

Do not work couching stitches too tightly

Make sure E and F are level

1 Come up at **A** and work a long horizontal stitch across to **B**. Bring the needle out level with **A**, at **C**.

2 Make a couching stitch: take the needle over the long stitch and insert at **D**. Draw the thread up gently to tighten. Come out at **E**, ready to make the next couching stitch.

········· STITCH VARIATION ·········

Bokhara couching is worked in the same way, but the couching stitches are much shorter and made at a steep angle.

Spiral Couching

Work first round of couching stitches at right angles

Make sure laid threads cover fabric completely

Lay threads in a clockwise spiral

1 Mark a circle and bring the couching thread up just above the center, at **A**. Fold the laid thread in half, pass the needle through the loop and insert at **B** to make a couching stitch. Curve the threads to the right. Work three more stitches, to complete the round. Make another round of four couching stitches.

2 Continue couching the laid threads in a spiral, spacing the stitches further apart as it increases in diameter. Take the ends through to the back to finish.

Couched Filling

········ LEVEL ········
Intermediate

········· USES ···········
Decorative open filling

········ METHOD ········
*Straight stitch grid with
cross stitch couching*

······ MATERIALS ······
*Any fabric; thread in
two colors of the same
or different
thickness; frame*

*Work upright stitches at right
angles to horizontal stitches*

*Be sure stitches
are parallel and
spaced evenly*

*Keep cross stitches small
for neat appearance*

1 Using the first color, make a foundation of horizontal straight stitches (see p.73). Come up at **A** to start working the vertical stitches. Take the needle down at **B**, then bring it out at **C**. Insert at **D** and come out at **E**, ready for the final stitch.

2 Work a cross stitch over each intersection of the straight stitches. Bring the second color up at **F**. Take the needle down over the crossed threads and insert at **G**. Come up at **H** and insert at **I**, then come out at **J**, ready to make the next cross.

Laid Trellis

········ LEVEL ········
Advanced

········· USES ···········
Decorative solid filling

········ METHOD ········
*Surface satin stitch with
trellis of couched straight
stitches*

······ MATERIALS ······
*Any fabric; thread in
three colors; frame*

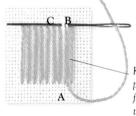

*Keep stitches
parallel so no
fabric shows
through*

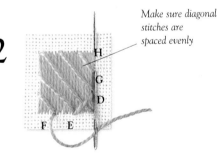

*Make sure diagonal
stitches are
spaced evenly*

*Work tie stitches over
crossed threads*

1 Work a row of upright surface satin stitches (see p.86), leaving one stitch width between each. Bring the needle out at **A**, insert at **B** and come up at **C**. Repeat along the row to fill in the spaces.

2 Using the second color of thread, work a series of diagonal stitches across the foundation. Come up at **D** to start the second layer of stitches. Take the needle down at **E**, then bring it out at **F** and insert at **G**. Come out at **H**, ready to complete the trellis.

3 Work the short tie stitches (see p.20) in the third color. Come up at **I**, take the needle down at **J** and bring it out again at **K**. Repeat at each intersection.

Back Stitch Trellis

········ LEVEL ········
Intermediate

········ USES ·········
Open geometric filling

······· METHOD ········
*Intersecting diagonal rows
of back stitch*

······ MATERIALS ·······
*Any fabric – evenweave
for a regular effect; any
embroidery thread*

*Space lines one stitch
length apart*

1

*Work stitches into
holes made by
previous row*

2

*Stitch at right
angles to
previous row*

1 Work a series of diagonal, parallel rows of back stitch (see p.40). Start the first row at **A**, the second at **B** and the third at **C**. Come out at **D**, insert the needle at **E** and bring it out at **F**. Continue until the required area is filled.

2 Work the next row in the opposite direction, starting at **C**, then **G**. Come out at **H**, insert at **I** and come up at **J**. Repeat to complete the trellis.

Japanese Darning

········ LEVEL ·········
Intermediate

·········· USES ··········
*Open geometric filling
for larger areas*

········ METHOD ········
*Combination of running
and straight stitches*

······· MATERIALS ·······
*Any fabric – evenweave
is easier to use; any
embroidery thread*

*Work running stitch
in parallel rows*

1

2

*Work slanting stitches
into holes made by
running stitches*

*Make sure
stitches are
longer than
spaces*

1 Work several horizontal rows of running stitch (see p.39), positioned so that the stitches in each row lie beneath the spaces in the row above. Come up at **A**, insert the needle at **B** and bring it out at **C**. Repeat to fill the required area.

2 Link the rows of running stitch with slanting stitches. Bring the needle out at **D** and take it down at **E**. Come up at **C**, go down at **F**, then up at **G**, ready to make the next stitch. Continue to the end of the row, before proceeding to the one below.

Cloud Filling

Position each stitch between two in row above

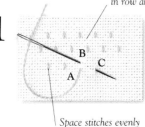

1

B C
A

Space stitches evenly

2

D

Use blunt needle for lacing

3

E

····· OTHER NAME ·····
Mexican stitch

········ LEVEL ········
Intermediate

········ USES ········
Open filling; crewel work

······· METHOD ·······
Interlaced rows of short upright stitches

····· MATERIALS ·····
Any fabric – evenweave for regular effect; any thread in two colors; blunt needle

1 Work a foundation of short upright stitches, arranged in staggered rows. Come up at **A** and make a straight stitch to **B**, then bring the needle out at **C**. Repeat to fill the required area.

2 Bring the second thread up at **D**. Slide the needle under the first stitch in the top row from left to right. Pass it beneath the second stitch on the row below and continue lacing to the end.

3 Come up at **E**. Slide the needle under the first stitch on the third row, from right to left. Take it under the next stitch on the second row. Repeat to the end, then thread further rows in the same way.

Wave Filling

2

1

C B A

Pick up a small amount of fabric with needle

F
D E

C

Needle passes under two threads

········ LEVEL ········
Intermediate

········ USES ········
Shaded or single color open filling; crewel work

······· METHOD ·······
Interlinked horizontal rows of looped stitches

····· MATERIALS ·····
Any fabric; any thread in one or more colors; frame

1 Work a base row of short, evenly spaced upright stitches. Come up at **A** and slide the needle under the first stitch. Take it back down to **B** and insert. Come out just to the left, at **C** and repeat to the end of the row.

2 Start the next row at **D**. Pass the needle under the next two stitches of the row above. Take it down and insert at **E**, then come out at **F**. Continue to the end of the row.

········ TECHNIQUE VARIATION ········

Create a subtly shaded effect by stitching each successive row in a darker shade of the same color.

OPENWORK

PULLED FABRIC STITCHES

· · · · · · · · · ◆ · · · · · · · ·

DRAWN THREAD AND
INSERTION STITCHES

· · · · · · · · · ◆ · · · · · · · ·

CUTWORK AND
EDGING STITCHES

Pulled Fabric Stitches

M ANY OF THESE stitches were originally worked as white-on-white stitches to decorate household linen, but their diversity and intricate patterns become more apparent when colored threads are used. They form all-over designs which vary in density; some are open and lacy, but others have a more solid pattern of stitches. Work on evenweave fabric which has been mounted in a frame. Avoid stretching the fabric too taut; it has to be fairly loose to allow the stitches to be worked evenly. Use strong thread in a weight to match the background fabric and pull each stitch tightly to draw the fabric threads together.

Window Filling

········ LEVEL ·········
Easy

··········· USES ···········
Dense filling

········· METHOD ·········
*Diamond trellis with
four small holes*

········· MATERIALS ·······
*Evenweave fabric;
any thread; blunt
needle; frame*

1

*Pull thread tightly to
create holes*

1 Come up at **A**. Work a diagonal stitch over five horizontal and two vertical threads, down to **B**. Come out five threads to the left, at **C**, then insert one thread to the left of **A**, at **D**. Bring the needle out five threads to the left, at **E** and go down one thread to the left of **C**, at **F**. Come out at **G** and continue to the end of the row.

2 Stitch the next row as a mirror image of the first. Come up at **H**, eleven threads below **E**, and insert one thread below **G**, at **I**. Repeat these two rows to continue.

*Count threads
carefully when
stitching*

2

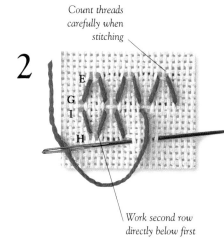

*Work second row
directly below first*

········· STITCH VARIATION·········

Pulled wave filling, which has open holes, is worked in the same way, but no space is left between the stitches.

Three-sided

····· OTHER NAME ·····
Straight line stitch

··········· LEVEL ···········
Easy

··········· USES ···········
Narrow borders

········· METHOD ·········
*Double back stitch
worked in triangles*

······· MATERIALS ·······
*Evenweave fabric;
any thread;
blunt needle; frame*

*Draw thread up
tightly to form holes*

1

2

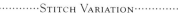

1 Start at **A** and work a diagonal stitch over six horizontal and three vertical threads down to **B**. Come out again at **A** and re-insert at **B** to make a double back stitch. Come up six threads to the left of **B**, at **C**, and work another double back stitch.

2 Work another double back stitch up to **A** and come out six threads to the left, at **D**.

3 Take the needle down to **C** and make a double stitch. Repeat to the end of the row.

3

Honeycomb Filling

Work each stitch over three threads

1

Make sure stitches are all worked at right angles to each other

2

Make a double horizontal stitch at point where rows meet

········ LEVEL ········
Intermediate

········· USES ·········
Light filling with semi-open appearance

······· METHOD ·······
Worked to form hexagonal lattice

····· MATERIALS ·····
Evenweave fabric; any thread; blunt needle

1 Start at top right. Come up at **A**, go down at **B** and bring the needle out at **C**. Re-insert at **B** and come up again at **C**, then go down at **D**. Come up at **E**, re-insert the needle at **D**, and bring it out again at **E**. Repeat these four stitches to the end of the row.

2 Work the second row as a mirror image of the first. Start at **F**, and turn the work upside-down if desired. Repeat these two rows to fill the required area.

Russian Filling

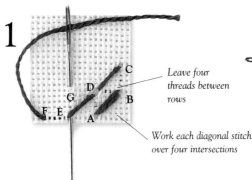

1

Leave four threads between rows

Work each diagonal stitch over four intersections

2

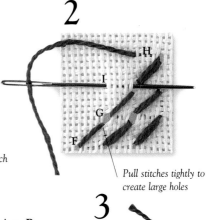

Pull stitches tightly to create large holes

3

········ LEVEL ········
Advanced

········· USES ·········
Dense filling with open holes

······· METHOD ·······
Crossed diagonal stitches worked in two journeys

····· MATERIALS ·····
Evenweave fabric; any thread; blunt needle

1 Start at bottom right. Work a diagonal stitch from **A** to **B**. Come up at **C** and insert the needle at **D**. Bring it back up at **B**, down at **A**, then up again at **D** and down at **E**. Start the next row with a stitch from **F** to **G** and come up at **E**. Repeat these two rows until the top right corner of the area being filled is reached.

2 Work a stitch from **H** to **I** to square off the top edge, then continue working diagonal rows to fill the space.

3 The second journey, which completes the crosses, starts from **J** to **H**. Turn the work through 45 degrees to the left and stitch as before.

Diagonal Raised Band

········· LEVEL ·········
Easy

·········· USES ··········
Ridged diagonal borders

········ METHOD ········
*Diagonal row of tightly
worked cross stitches*

······ MATERIALS ······
*Evenweave fabric; any
thread; blunt needle;
frame*

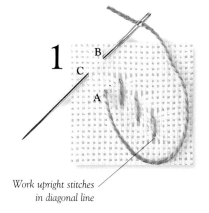

*Work upright stitches
in diagonal line*

*Pull thread
up firmly*

1 Work a row of upright stitches. Come out at **A**, take the needle up over six threads and insert it at **B**. Bring the needle out three intersections to the left, at **C**.

2 Insert the needle at **D** and bring it out again at **A**. Insert at **E** and come out at **F**, and continue to the end of the row.

········ STITCH VARIATION ········

Ridged filling is made by working diagonal raised band stitch in adjacent rows to make a solid pattern.

Punch

········· LEVEL ··········
Easy

·········· USES ··········
*Open filling with large
holes*

········ METHOD ········
*Double back stitch worked
in square grid*

······ MATERIALS ······
*Evenweave fabric; any
thread; blunt needle;
frame*

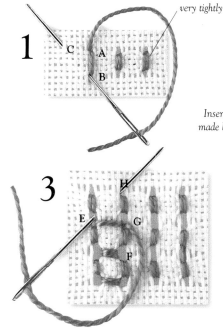

*Work double stitches
very tightly*

*Insert needle into hole
made by previous stitch*

1 Come up at **A** and work an upright stitch over four threads to **B**. Make a second stitch in the same holes, then come out five intersections to the left, at **C**. Repeat to the end of the row.

2 Bring the needle out five threads below the final stitch, at **D**. Work a double back stitch between **D** and **E**, then come up five threads to the right, at **F**. Continue to the end of the row then repeat to fill the required area.

3 Work horizontal stitches between the upright rows. Come up at **G** and make a double back stitch to **E**. Bring the needle out at **H**, then continue working up and down the rows.

Cobbler Filling

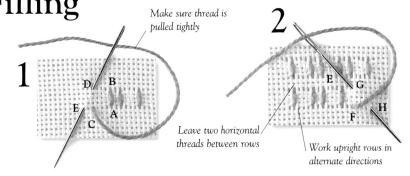

Make sure thread is pulled tightly

Leave two horizontal threads between rows

Work upright rows in alternate directions

.... LEVEL ....
Intermediate

.... USES ....
Light, open filling

.... METHOD ....
Straight stitches worked in vertical and horizontal rows to form pattern of detached squares

.... MATERIALS ....
Evenweave fabric; any thread; blunt needle; frame

1 Come up at **A** and take the needle up over four threads to **B**. Bring it out four threads to the left of **A** at **C**. Insert at **D** and come up two threads to the left of **C** at **E**. Repeat to the end of the row.

2 Work the following rows of upright stitches in line with the first. Bring the needle up six threads below the previous stitch, at **F**. Insert at **G** and come up at **H**.

3 Join the pairs of stitches to form squares. Bring the needle up at **D**, take it down at **B** and up at **C**. Insert at **A**, then continue working down and up the rows.

Step

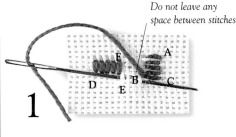

Do not leave any space between stitches

Make sure blocks meet at each corner

Work each satin stitch over four threads

.... LEVEL ....
Intermediate

.... USES ....
Dense filling

.... METHOD ....
Diagonal rows made up of blocks of satin stitch set at alternate angles

.... MATERIALS ....
Evenweave fabric; any thread; blunt needle; frame

1 Start at **A**. Work a block of five horizontal stitches over four threads, ending with **B** to **C**. Come up eight threads to the left of **B**, at **D**. Work five upright stitches over four threads, ending with **E** to **F**. Come out at **B**, insert at **E** and work four more horizontal stitches.

2 Come up eight threads below **B**, at **G**. Insert at **H** work four more upright satin stitches.

3 Bring the needle out eight threads below **G**, at **I**. Work five stitches over four threads, ending at **J**. Come up at **G** to make a block of upright stitches. Continue making alternate blocks to fill the required area.

Mosaic Filling

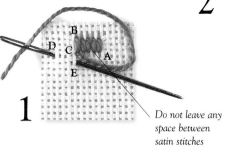

Do not leave any space between satin stitches

1

Make sure all satin stitches are worked over four threads

2

Pull back stitches tightly

3

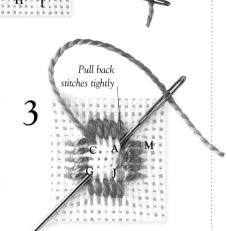

.... LEVEL ....
Advanced

.... USES ....
Dense chequered filling

.... METHOD ....
Block of satin stitch set in a square with back stitch center

.... MATERIALS ....
Evenweave fabric; any thread; blunt needle; frame

1 Start at **A**. Work five satin stitches (see p.86) over four threads, finishing at **B**. Come out at **C**. Insert four threads to the left, at **D**, and come out at **E**.

2 Work four more horizontal stitches, finishing at **F**. Come up at **G** and insert the needle four threads below, at **H**. Work four more upright stitches, ending at **I**. Come up at **J**, insert at **K** and come out at **L**.

3 Work four more stitches, ending at **M**. Come back up at **A** and insert at **J**. Work three more back stitches from **C** to **A**, **G** to **C** and **J** to **G** to complete. Start the next stitch to the left (see Gallery p.31).

Diagonal Satin Filling

Leave five vertical threads between rows

Pull stitches tightly to create diamond

1

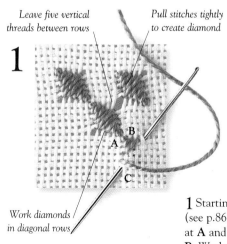

Work diamonds in diagonal rows

2

Stitch into holes made by previous blocks

.... LEVEL ....
Intermediate

.... USES ....
Dense geometric filling

.... METHOD ....
Diagonal rows of satin stitch diamonds, worked in alternate directions

.... MATERIALS ....
Evenweave fabric; any thread; blunt needle; frame

1 Starting at top right, work a series of satin stitch (see p.86) diamonds to fill the required area. Come up at **A** and make a diagonal stitch over one intersection to **B**. Work four more stitches, increasing the length of each by one thread. Come up at **C** to work the longest stitch, then complete the diamond with four stitches which decrease in size.

2 Fill in the spaces with further rows of diamonds worked in the same way but in the opposite direction.

Ringed Back Stitch Filling

*Stitch return journey
in opposite direction*

········· LEVEL ·········
Intermediate

········· USES ·········
Filling for large areas

········ METHOD ········
*Intersecting rows of back
stitch forming pattern of
small circles*

······· MATERIALS ·······
*Evenweave fabric; any
thread; blunt needle;
frame*

1 Start at **A** and take the needle down over two intersections, at **B**. Come up two threads above **A**, at **C**, then continue working alternate straight and diagonal back stitches to form a row of semi-circles.

2 Work a full circle at the end of the row. The lines cross at the upright stitches; work a second back stitch between **E** and **D**, then continue stitching from right to left.

3 Come up at **F** to start the next row. Work from left to right, making a second horizontal stitch between **G** and **H**, and at each point where two rows meet.

*Work each back stitch
over two vertical threads*

Algerian Eye

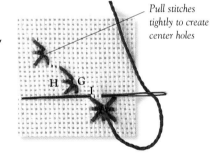

*Pull stitches
tightly to create
center holes*

*Work stitches
over three
vertical
threads*

········· LEVEL ·········
Intermediate

········· USES ·········
*Checkerboard filling for
large areas*

········ METHOD ········
*Straight stitch stars
worked in two journeys*

······· MATERIALS ·······
*Evenweave fabric; any
thread; blunt needle;
frame*

1 Start at **A** and take the needle down over three intersections, at **B**. Come up three threads to the left, at **C** and insert at **B**. Bring the needle up at **D**, down at **B**, up at **E** and down at **B**. Come out three threads to the right of **E**, at **F**. For the next half star, go down over three intersections, at **G**, and up at **H**.

2 Continue stitching downward, working half stars to fill the required area. Complete the final star with four more straight stitches, finishing at **I**. Insert at **G** to continue the second journey.

3 Come up at **J**, six threads to the right of the top star, ready to work the next diagonal row of stars.

Outlined Diamond Eyelet

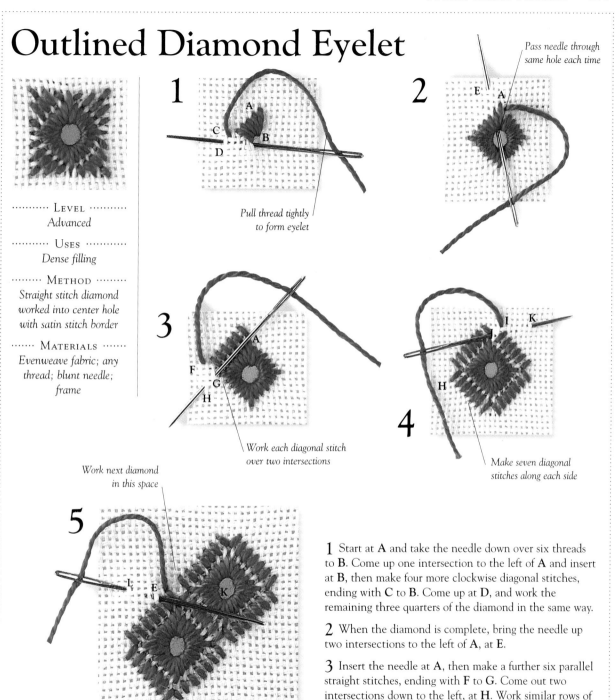

Pass needle through same hole each time

Pull thread tightly to form eyelet

Work each diagonal stitch over two intersections

Make seven diagonal stitches along each side

Work next diamond in this space

········· LEVEL ·········
Advanced

········· USES ·········
Dense filling

········ METHOD ········
Straight stitch diamond worked into center hole with satin stitch border

······· MATERIALS ·······
Evenweave fabric; any thread; blunt needle; frame

1 Start at **A** and take the needle down over six threads to **B**. Come up one intersection to the left of **A** and insert at **B**, then make four more clockwise diagonal stitches, ending with **C** to **B**. Come up at **D**, and work the remaining three quarters of the diamond in the same way.

2 When the diamond is complete, bring the needle up two intersections to the left of **A**, at **E**.

3 Insert the needle at **A**, then make a further six parallel straight stitches, ending with **F** to **G**. Come out two intersections down to the left, at **H**. Work similar rows of straight stitch along the other three sides.

4 Make the final stitch from **I** to **J**. Come up six threads to the right, at **K**, and repeat steps 1 to 3 to work the next diamond.

5 To work the next diamond to the left, come back up at **E** and take the needle down six threads to the left, at **L**.

Drawn Thread and Insertion Stitches

DRAWN THREAD HEM and border stitches developed as a method of producing a decorative neatened edge on a piece of fabric. They should be worked on evenweave fabric from which a band of threads has been withdrawn. The remaining threads are then bunched together with tightly pulled stitches to form a regular pattern. Insertion stitches, also known as faggoting, have developed from old seaming techniques into a group of intricate stitches, which can be worked on plain or evenweave fabric. The two edges being joined must be mounted on paper so that the stitches can be spaced evenly.

Hem

····· OTHER NAME ·····
Single hem stitch

········· LEVEL ·········
Easy

·········· USES ··········
Border for hemmed edge

········ METHOD ········
Thread groups pulled into clusters along hem; worked on wrong side of fabric

······ MATERIALS ······
Evenweave fabric; any thread; blunt needle

1

Work on wrong side of fabric

2 Pull thread tightly to bunch threads

Work each stitch over same number of threads

1 Pull out a few threads along the edge of the fabric (see p.21). Fold a double hem to the edge of the threads and tack down. Come up at **A** and slide the needle under three threads to the right, from **B** to **C**.

2 Take the needle down at **B** and bring it out at **D**. Repeat these two steps to continue.

········ STITCH VARIATION ········

Ladder hem stitch is worked over a wider band of pulled threads. Work as for hem stitch, then turn the fabric upside down and work a second row over the same groups of threads, making a series of bars.

Serpentine Hem

····· OTHER NAME ·····
Trellis hem stitch

········· LEVEL ·········
Easy

·········· USES ··········
Decorative edging

········ METHOD ········
Two staggered rows of hem stitch worked to create slanting bars

······ MATERIALS ······
Evenweave fabric; any thread; blunt needle

Withdraw several threads to create wide band

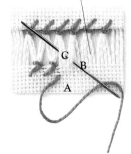

Work a row of hem stitch over groups of four threads (see above), then turn the fabric upside down. Come up at **A**. Pass the needle under two threads from each group, from **B** to **C**, and work a second row of hem stitch.

Antique Hem

········· LEVEL ·········
Easy

·········· USES ··········
Plain border for hem

········ METHOD ········
Hem stitch variation in which horizontal stitches only show on right side

······ MATERIALS ······
Evenweave fabric; any thread; blunt needle

Pass needle through folded hem

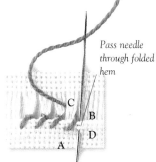

Prepare the fabric as for hem stitch (see above). With the wrong side facing, come up at **A**. Slide the needle under three threads to the right, from **B** to **C**. Insert the needle through the edge of the fold at **B** and come out at **D**. Pull up the thread; repeat this step to continue.

Italian Border

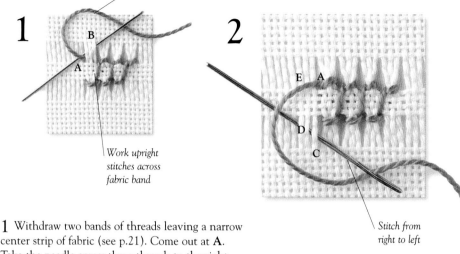

Draw up loop to pull threads together

1

Work upright stitches across fabric band

2

Stitch from right to left

···· OTHER NAME ····
Italian hem stitch

········ LEVEL ········
Easy

········ USES ········
Open band; with hem stitch as decorative border

······· METHOD ·······
Open border stitch, worked in two journeys

····· MATERIALS ·····
Evenweave fabric; any thread; blunt needle

1 Withdraw two bands of threads leaving a narrow center strip of fabric (see p.21). Come out at **A**. Take the needle across three threads to the right and then slide it behind the fabric from **B** to **A**.

2 Take the needle down to **C**. Slide it behind three threads and come out at **D**. Go back down at **C** and come up at **E**, three threads to the left of **A**. Repeat steps 1 and 2 to continue.

Four-sided

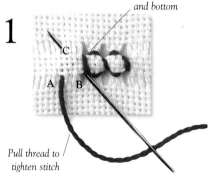

Work over same threads at top and bottom

1

Pull thread to tighten stitch

Insert needle alternately from left to right

2

········ LEVEL ········
Intermediate

········ USES ········
Open bands; can also be worked as pulled fabric stitch

······· METHOD ·······
Pulled straight stitches, worked horizontally to form square pattern

····· MATERIALS ·····
Evenweave fabric; any thread; blunt needle

1 Withdraw two bands of threads leaving a narrow strip of fabric between them (see p.21). Come up at **A**. Take the needle down four threads to the right, at **B**. Bring it out directly above **A**, at **C**.

2 Take the needle down four threads to the right, at **D** and come up at **A**. Go down at **C** to make a vertical stitch and come up four threads to the left of **A**, ready to start the next stitch. Repeat these two steps to continue.

Chevron Border

·········· **Level** ··········
Intermediate

·········· **Uses** ··········
Decorative open bands; with hem stitch as edging

········ **Method** ········
Chevron stitch variation; worked horizontally

······ **Materials** ······
Evenweave fabric; any thread; blunt needle

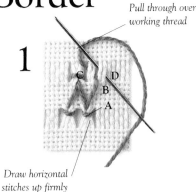

Pull through over working thread

Draw horizontal stitches up firmly

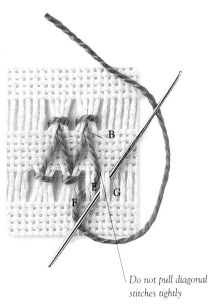

Do not pull diagonal stitches tightly

1 Prepare the fabric as for step 1 below. Come up at **A**. Take the needle diagonally up and slide it behind two threads from **B** to **C**. Take the needle across four threads to the right, and insert at **D**. Come up again at **B**.

2 Insert the needle at **E**. Slide it behind two threads to the left and come up at **F**. Take the needle across four threads and insert at **G**. Bring it out at **E** and pull through over the working thread. Repeat these two steps to the end of the row.

Diamond Border

·········· **Level** ··········
Intermediate

·········· **Uses** ··········
Open border with hexagonal pattern

········ **Method** ········
Pulled straight stitches, worked in two journeys

······ **Materials** ······
Evenweave fabric; any thread; blunt needle

Work each horizontal stitch over same number of threads

Pull horizontal stitches tightly

Work second journey as mirror image of first

1 Withdraw two bands of thread leaving a narrow strip of fabric between them (see p.21). Come up in the center, at **A**. Take the needle down three threads to the right, at **B**, then bring it out at **A** again. Insert directly above, at **C** and slide the needle under three threads to the left, coming up at **D**.

2 Take the needle down at **C** and come back up at **D**. Insert it directly below, at **E** and come out on the same level, at **F**. Repeat steps 1 and 2 to the end of the row.

3 Turn the fabric the other way up to work the second journey. Come up at **G** and stitch as before.

Laced Insertion

Keep tension regular

····· OTHER NAME ·····
Laced faggot stitch

········· LEVEL ·········
Easy

········· USES ·········
Decorative joining stitch

········ METHOD ········
Two hems worked with Antwerp edging stitch, linked with interlacing

······ MATERIALS ······
Evenweave fabric; thick thread; blunt needle

Mount the fabric (see p.21). Work a row of Antwerp edging stitch (see p.112) along each hem. Come up at **A**. Pass the needle down over **B**. Slide it under **C**, from back to front. Take it over **D**, from front to back; repeat to the end of the seam.

Cretan Insertion

········· LEVEL ·········
Easy

········· USES ·········
Simple join for two straight edges

········ METHOD ········
Open Cretan stitch adapted as insertion

······ MATERIALS ······
Evenweave fabric; thick thread; blunt needle

Mount the fabric on paper (see p.21). Take the needle through to the back at **A**, then insert it from the front at **B**. Bring it through behind the diagonal thread and take it down at **C**. Pull through over the working thread. Repeat to the end of the seam.

Insertion Bundles

········· LEVEL ·········
Intermediate

········· USES ·········
Decorative method of joining two edges

········ METHOD ········
Groups of two stitches bound by a third, worked from top to bottom

······ MATERIALS ······
Evenweave fabric; any thread; blunt needle

Loop thread from left to right

1 Mount the fabric on paper (see p.21). Start on the left, at **A** and work a straight stitch across to **B**, on the right. Make another stitch from **C** to **D**, then come out at **E**. Pass the needle behind all the threads, then pull through over the loop.

Pull thread tightly to bunch stitches

2 Insert the needle at **F**, then bring it out below **E** at **G**, ready to start the next group of stitches.

Leave equal spaces between all stitches

Maintain even tension

3 Insert at **H**, then make another stitch from **I** to **J**. Come out at **K**, take the needle behind the three diagonal and two horizontal threads, and pull through over the working thread. Repeat steps 1 to 3 to continue.

Knotted Insertion

····· OTHER NAME ·····
Knotted faggot stitch

········ LEVEL ········
Advanced

········· USES ·········
Decorative method of joining two edges

······· METHOD ·······
Knotted joining stitch worked horizontally

······ MATERIALS ······
Evenweave fabric; thick thread; blunt needle

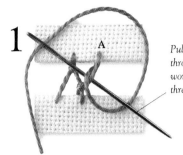

Pull needle through over working thread

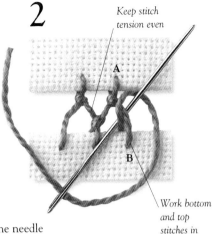

Keep stitch tension even

Work bottom and top stitches in same way

1 Mount the fabric on paper (see p.21). Take the needle down through the top hem at **A** and bring it out to the left of the diagonal stitch. Loop the working thread to the right and pass the needle under both threads. Pull the thread up tightly to form a knot.

2 Take the needle down to the bottom hem and insert at **B**. Bring it through to the left of the diagonal stitch and loop the thread to the right. Slide the needle under both threads and pull through tightly. Continue stitching alternately up and down to the end of the seam.

Buttonhole Insertion

····· OTHER NAME ·····
Buttonhole faggot stitch

········ LEVEL ········
Advanced

········· USES ·········
Decorative joining method

······· METHOD ·······
Groups of three button-hole stitches worked alternately from top to bottom

······ MATERIALS ······
Evenweave fabric; thick thread; blunt needle

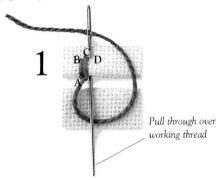

Pull through over working thread

Make small diagonal stitch between two hems

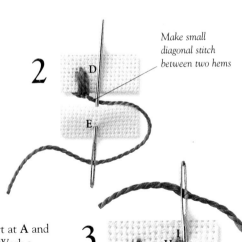

Work longest stitch in center

1 Mount the fabric on paper (see p.21). Start at **A** and work a buttonhole stitch (see p.58) up to **B**. Work a second, longer stitch to **C**, then come out on the same level as **B**, at **D**, to work the third stitch.

2 Take the needle down through the bottom hem, at **E** and pull it through over the working thread.

3 Work two more buttonhole stitches at **F** and **G**, varying the length as before, then take the needle back up to the top hem at **H**. Make two more stitches at **I** and **J**, then continue to the end of the seam.

Needleweaving Bars

Work each bar over even number of threads

1

C A B

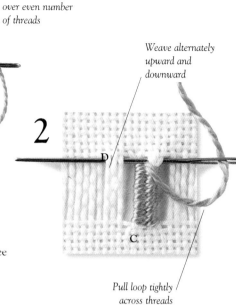

Weave alternately upward and downward

2

D

C

Pull loop tightly across threads

····· OTHER NAME ·····
Woven bars

········· LEVEL ·········
Advanced

········· USES ·········
Flat, heavy borders

········ METHOD ········
Weaving stitch, worked horizontally

······ MATERIALS ······
Evenweave fabric; any thread; blunt needle

1 Withdraw a band of threads from the fabric. (see p.21). Come up at **A** and take the needle across three threads to the right. Insert it at **B** and bring it back through at **A**. Insert over three threads to the left at **C**, then come back out in the center, at **A**. Continue weaving upward.

2 When the bar is complete, bring the needle out three threads to the left, at **D**. Work downward as before, then continue weaving bars to the end of the row.

Zigzag Clusters

Pull double stitch tightly

1

B   C

A

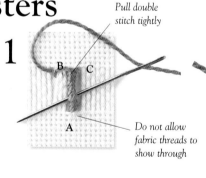

Do not allow fabric threads to show through

Join clusters at the top

2

C

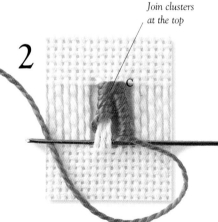

········· LEVEL ·········
Advanced

·········· USES ··········
Heavy open borders

········ METHOD ········
Round, wrapped bars worked over foundation of drawn threads

······ MATERIALS ······
Evenweave fabric; any thread; blunt needle

1 Withdraw a band of threads (see p.21). Start at **A** and take the needle over three threads to the right. Come back up at **A**, then pass the needle in front of and behind the threads. Continue wrapping to the top, then come out three threads to the left, at **B**. Take the needle across six threads and insert at **C**, then come back up at **B**. Insert again at **C** and come up between the two groups of threads.

2 Take the needle back over three threads and continue wrapping to the bottom. Start the next and subsequent clusters three threads to the left.

···········STITCH VARIATION···········

Corded clusters are worked in the same way, but without the double linking stitches.

Cutwork and Edging Stitches

Edging stitches give an ornamental finish to a hem and look particularly effective when worked in a thick, twisted thread. The stitches should be spaced regularly, but they can be worked on evenweave or plainweave fabric. Cutwork stitches, like the other types of openwork, were grouped under the name of 'white work'. Eyelets in various shapes can be used to decorate collars, mats, and garments or combined with satin stitch to create *Broderie Anglaise* designs on lawn. Work these stitches on fine plainweave cotton or linen, in white or colored threads, with or without a frame.

Antwerp Edging

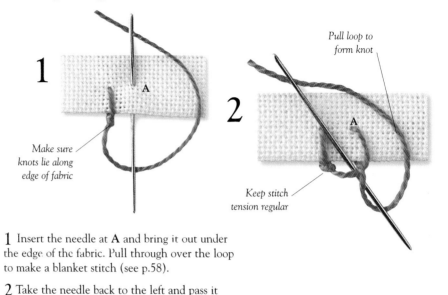

··· **OTHER NAME** ···
Knotted blanket stitch

······ **LEVEL** ······
Intermediate

····· **USES** ·····
Decorative hems

····· **METHOD** ·····
*Blanket stitch variation,
worked horizontally over
edge of fabric*

····· **MATERIALS** ·····
*Any fabric; thick twisted
threads give best
stitch definition*

*Make sure
knots lie along
edge of fabric*

*Pull loop to
form knot*

*Keep stitch
tension regular*

1 Insert the needle at **A** and bring it out under
the edge of the fabric. Pull through over the loop
to make a blanket stitch (see p.58).

2 Take the needle back to the left and pass it
behind the two threads. Draw up the working
thread to form a knot. Repeat these two steps to
continue along the edge.

Sailor Edging

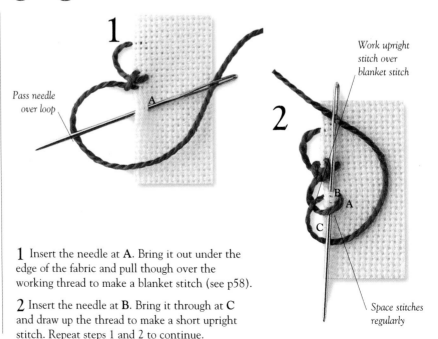

······ **LEVEL** ······
Intermediate

····· **USES** ·····
Decorative hems

····· **METHOD** ·····
*Blanket stitch variation,
worked downward over
edge of fabric*

····· **MATERIALS** ·····
*Any fabric; any twisted
thread*

*Pass needle
over loop*

*Work upright
stitch over
blanket stitch*

*Space stitches
regularly*

1 Insert the needle at **A**. Bring it out under the
edge of the fabric and pull though over the
working thread to make a blanket stitch (see p58).

2 Insert the needle at **B**. Bring it through at **C**
and draw up the thread to make a short upright
stitch. Repeat steps 1 and 2 to continue.

Looped Edge

.... LEVEL ....
Intermediate

.... USES ....
Solid stitch for hems and neatening raw edges; foundation for laced insertion stitch

.... METHOD ....
Looped edging stitch, worked horizontally

...... MATERIALS ......
Any fabric; any thread depending on fabric

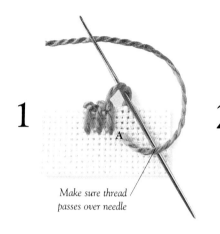

1 *Make sure thread passes over needle*

Work stitches closely together to conceal edge

Keep stitches same length

1 Come up at **A**. Take the needle to the left and pass it downward through the loop. Pull up the thread gently.

2 Bring the needle out at **B**, ready to make the next stitch. Repeat these two steps to continue.

Half Chevron

.... LEVEL ....
Intermediate

.... USES ....
To neaten folded edges and hems

.... METHOD ....
Chevron stitch variation, worked over edge of fabric

...... MATERIALS ......
Any fabric; any thread

1 *Keep needle horizontal*

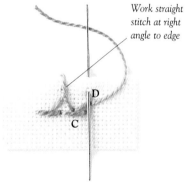

2 *Work straight stitch at right angle to edge*

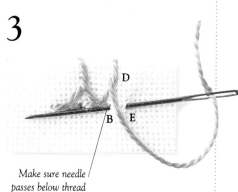

3 *Make sure needle passes below thread*

1 Come up at **A**, insert the needle at **B**, and bring it out in the center, at **C**.

2 Loop the thread from left to right. Take the needle behind the fabric and bring it through over the working thread, at **D**.

3 Insert the needle to the right of **B**, at **E**, then bring it through again at **B**. Repeat steps 1 to 3 to continue along the edge.

Scalloped Edge

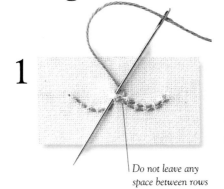

*Do not leave any
space between rows*

1 Sew two foundation rows of closely spaced running stitch (see p.39) along the outline of the edge to be worked.

2 Work a row of buttonhole stitch (see p.58) over the foundation, following the curve of the outline. Come up at **A**, insert at **B**, and pull the needle through at **C**. Repeat to the end of the line. When the stitching is complete, trim away the surplus fabric using sharp embroidery scissors.

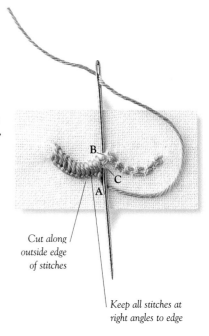

*Cut along
outside edge
of stitches*

*Keep all stitches at
right angles to edge*

Ring Picot Edge

*Pull needle
through to make
buttonhole stitch*

*Do not pull stitches
too tightly*

1 Sew a line of closely spaced running stitch (see p.39) along the edge to be worked. Make a row of buttonhole stitch (see p.58) over it, finishing at the right edge of the picot, at **A**. Take the needle back to **B** and pass it under the horizontal thread to form the foundation loop. Slide the needle under the loop from right to left, over the working thread and gently pull through.

2 Work a series of buttonhole stitches to cover the foundation loop.

3 Continue working buttonhole stitch along the marked line. When complete, carefully trim away the surplus fabric using sharp embroidery scissors.

Buttonhole Eyelet

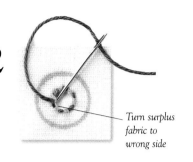

Reinforce opening with running stitch

Turn surplus fabric to wrong side

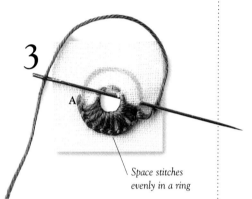

Space stitches evenly in a ring

········ LEVEL ········
Advanced

········· USES ··········
Circular holes; laced eyelets

······· METHOD ········
Buttonhole stitch worked in a ring around central opening

······ MATERIALS ·······
Closely woven fabric; any fine thread; sharp scissors

1 Mark two concentric circles on the fabric. Outline the inner circle with a round of closely spaced running stitch (see p.39).

2 Clip the knot and make two cuts at right angles across the inner circle. Using the point of the needle, ease the fabric to the wrong side and finger press in place.

3 Come up at **A** on the outer circle and work a circle of buttonhole stitch (see p.58) into the center. Trim any surplus fabric on the wrong side.

Overcast Eyelet

Do not leave any space between stitches

········ LEVEL ········
Advanced

········· USES ··········
Broderie Anglaise; openwork

······· METHOD ········
Small open circle with bound edge

······ MATERIALS ·······
Fine cotton or linen; any fine thread

Draw a circle onto the fabric and prepare as for steps 1 and 2 above. Bring the needle up a short distance away from the folded edge, at **A**, and work a ring of short stitches into the space.

Square Eyelet

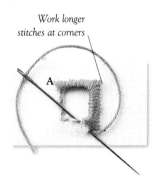

Work longer stitches at corners

········ LEVEL ········
Advanced

········· USES ··········
Broderie Anglaise; openwork

······· METHOD ········
Cut square with bound edge

······ MATERIALS ·······
Any fine fabric; fine thread

Mark the outline and work a round of running stitch over it. Make two diagonal cuts across the square and finger press the surplus fabric to the wrong side. Come up at **A** and work a round of straight stitches into the opening, angling them at each corner.

Needlepoint

Straight Needlepoint Stitches

· · · · · · · · ◆ · · · · · · · ·

Diagonal Needlepoint Stitches

· · · · · · · · ◆ · · · · · · · ·

Cross and Star
Needlepoint Stitches

· · · · · · · · ◆ · · · · · · · ·

Looped and Tied
Needlepoint Stitches

Straight Needlepoint Stitches

THIS VERSATILE GROUP of stitches includes stripes, zigzags, diamonds, and other geometric patterns which can be used for fillings and backgrounds on various scales, using one or more colors. They are all stitched either horizontally or vertically, so that the thread lies parallel to the grain of the canvas. This means that they do not distort the square weave in the same way as diagonal stitches, and, with care, they can be worked without a frame. The stitches are all sewn on single canvas, and the thread, yarn, or wool used must be thick enough to conceal the background completely.

Upright Gobelin

A B C D E F

*Work each
stitch over
four threads*

····· OTHER NAME ·····
Straight Gobelin stitch

········· LEVEL ·········
Easy

·········· USES ··········
*Ridged fillings and
backgrounds*

········· METHOD ·········
*Horizontal rows of vertical
straight stitches, worked
alternately from right to left*

····· MATERIALS ·····
Single canvas; any thread

Starting at top left, make an upright stitch from **5A** to **1A** and repeat to the end of the line. Begin the next row at **9F** to **5F** and stitch toward the left. Repeat these two rows to fill the required area.

Gobelin Filling

A B C D E F

*Work into base
of previous stitch*

········· LEVEL ·········
Easy

·········· USES ··········
*Twill effect backgrounds
and shaded fillings*

········· METHOD ·········
*Interlocking horizontal
rows of upright stitches*

······ MATERIALS ······
Single canvas; any thread

Start at top left. Work the first stitch from **7A** to **3A**, the second from **5B** to **1B** and repeat to the end of the line. Begin the next row at **9F** to **5F** and **11E** to **7E** and work toward the left; repeat these two rows to continue.

Parisian

········· LEVEL ·········
Easy

·········· USES ··········
*Textured fillings and large
background areas*

········· METHOD ·········
*Interlocking horizontal
rows of alternate long and
short upright stiches*

······ MATERIALS ······
Single canvas; any thread

1

A B   E F

*Work each row in
pairs of long and
short stitches*

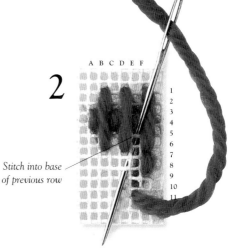

2

A B C D E F

*Stitch into base
of previous row*

1 Start at the top left corner. Work a short stitch over two threads from **5A** to **3A** and a long stitch over six threads from **7B** to **1B**. Repeat these two stitches to the end of the line.

2 Begin the next row with a short stitch from **9F** to **7F** and a long stitch from **11E** to **5E**, then work alternate long and short stitches to the end of the row. Repeat these two steps to fill the required area.

········· TECHNIQUE VARIATION ·········

To create a secondary pattern within Parisian stitch, work all the long stitches in a dark yarn, then fill the spaces with short stitches in a contrasting color.

Hungarian

·········· LEVEL ··········
Easy

·········· USES ··········
Textured fillings

········ METHOD ········
*Horizontal rows of small
interlocking diamonds*

······ MATERIALS ······
*Single canvas; any thread
in one or two colors*

*Work three
upright stitches to
make diamond*

1 Starting at top left, make a
short stitch over two threads from **4A** to **2A**.
Work a long stitch from **5B** to **1B**, then another
short stitch from **4C** to **2C**. Miss one space, then
come up at **4E** to start the next diamond.
Continue to the end of the line.

2 Using a contrasting color, come up at **6E** to
start the next row. Repeat the sequence of three
stitches and one space, working from right to left.

*Second row of stitches
is worked into spaces
below first row*

········ TECHNIQUE VARIATION ········

When Hungarian stitch
is worked in just a single
color it produces a
smooth, brocade-like
texture which provides a good background
for detailed tent stitch designs.

Hungarian Diamond

·········· LEVEL ··········
Easy

·········· USES ··········
*Striped backgrounds and
fillings*

········ METHOD ········
*Hungarian stitch variation
on larger scale*

······ MATERIALS ······
Single canvas; any thread

*Work progressively
longer and
shorter stitches*

*Stitch second row in
opposite direction,
working into spaces
left below first*

1 Start at top left. Work three progressively longer stitches from
5A to **3A**, **6B** to **2B** and **7C** to **1C**, then a shorter stitch from
6D to **2D**. Repeat these four stitches to the end of the row and
work two shorter stitches to complete the final diamond.

2 Use a second color for the next row. Start with a short stitch
from **9K** to **7K** and continue as above, working from right to left.
Repeat these two rows to fill the required area.

Single Twill

········ LEVEL ········
Easy

········ USES ·········
Ridged fillings and woven effect backgrounds

······· METHOD ·······
Diagonal rows of vertical straight stitches

····· MATERIALS ·····
Single canvas; any thread

Work each stitch a single thread higher than preceding stitch

Start at the top left with a straight stitch from **9A** to **5A**. Work the next from **8B** to **4B** and continue stitching upward. Start the next row at **9E** to **5E**, and continue working downward. Repeat these two rows to continue.

Double Twill

········ LEVEL ········
Easy

········ USES ·········
Textured fillings and backgrounds

······· METHOD ·······
Alternate rows of long and short upright stitches, worked diagonally

····· MATERIALS ·····
Single canvas; any thread

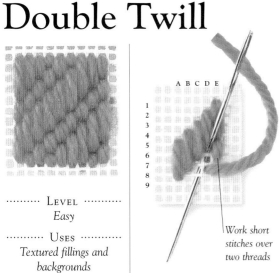

Work short stitches over two threads

Work the first row as for single twill stitch (see above). Start the second row with **7E** to **5E** and continue working short stitches downward. Repeat these two rows to fill the required area.

Bargello

····· OTHER NAMES ·····
Florentine stitch; flame stitch

········ LEVEL ········
Easy

········ USES ·········
Large patterned areas

······· METHOD ·······
Straight stitch worked in wide zigzag bands

····· MATERIALS ·····
Single canvas; any yarn in a selection of toning and contrasting colors

Insert needle into base of previous stitch

1 Start at the left with a straight stitch from **11A** to **7A**. Make three stitches upward from **9B** to **5B**, **7C** to **3C** and **5D** to **1D**. Work the next three stitches downward, leaving two threads between each, ending at **7G**. Come up at **9H** and repeat this sequence to the end of the row.

2 Stitch the next row in the same way, starting at **15A** and using a lighter shade of the same color. The third row is worked in a paler yarn, starting at **19A**. Repeat these three rows to continue.

········ TECHNIQUE VARIATION ········

To create a wider zigzag with a stepped effect, work blocks of two and three stitches in the center of the diagonals. Add in a contrasting color yarn to give more visual interest.

Chevron

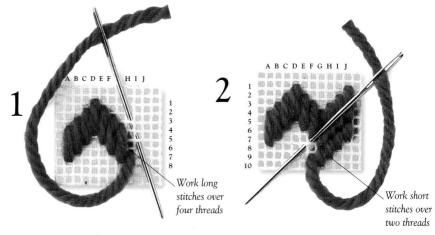

········· LEVEL ·········
Easy

·········· USES ··········
Backgrounds and fillings

········ METHOD ········
*Alternate zigzag bands of
long and short stitches*

······· MATERIALS ·······
*Single canvas; any thread
in one or two colors*

*Work long
stitches over
four threads*

*Work short
stitches over
two threads*

1 Start at the top left corner with a stitch from **8A** to **4A**. Work three more stitches upward from **7B** to **3B**, **6C** to **2C** and **5D** to **1D**, then two downward stitches from **6E** to **2E** and **7F** to **3F**. Repeat this sequence to the end of the row.

2 Begin the next row with a short stitch from **7J** to **5J**. Continue stitching from right to left, working into the base of the previous row. Repeat these two rows to continue.

········· TECHNIQUE VARIATION ·········
Emphasize the zigzag pattern within chevron stitch by working alternate rows in different color threads.

Hungarian Ground

········· LEVEL ·········
Intermediate

·········· USES ··········
Geometric fillings

········ METHOD ········
*Alternate straight stitch
zigzags and diamonds*

······· MATERIALS ·······
Single canvas; any thread

*Work diamond block of
four short stitches into
space below chevron*

*Work third row
as mirror image
of first*

1 Start at top left. Work three long stitches upward from **7A** to **3A**, **6B** to **2B** and **5C** to **1C** and one stitch downward from **6D** to **2D**, then repeat this block to the end of the line. Using the second color, make four short stitches from **8H** to **6H**, **7G** to **5G**, **9G** to **7G** and **8F** to **6F**. Start the next diamond at **8D**.

2 With the first color, work three stitches downward from **11I** to **7I**, **12H** to **8H** and **13G** to **9G**, then two stitches upward from **12F** to **8F** and **11E** to **7E**. Repeat to the end of the row; then fill in the spaces with diamonds.

Straight Cushion

········ LEVEL ········
Intermediate

········ USES ········
Checkerboard fillings

········ METHOD ········
*Alternate rows of
diamonds worked in long
and short straight stitches*

········ MATERIALS ········
*Single canvas; any thread
or yarn in two colors*

1

A B C D E F G H I

*Work three
diagonal rows
of three short
stitches*

*Stitch third row of
diamonds directly
below first diamonds*

2

A B C D E F G H I J

1 Work the first row as step 1 of Scottish diamond stitch (see below) starting at **5A**. Using a second color, work three rows of stitches, from **8H** to **6H**, **7G** to **5G**, **6F** to **4F**; **7E** to **5E**, **8F** to **6F**, **9G** to **7G** and **10F** to **8F**, **9E** to **7E** and **8D** to **6D**.

2 Work the third row as the first, starting at **11K** and stitching from right to left. Continue working alternate rows of dark and light diamonds.

········ TECHNIQUE VARIATION ········

Work straight cushion
stitch in two shades of
the same color, instead
of two contrasting yarns,
to give a subtle brocade
effect for fillings or large-scale backgrounds.

Scottish Diamond

········ LEVEL ········
Intermediate

········ USES ········
*Textured fillings and
backgrounds*

········ METHOD ········
*Straight stitch chevrons
and diamonds worked in
alternate rows*

········ MATERIALS ········
Single canvas; any thread

1

*Make five stitches
for each diamond*

A B C D E F G H I J K L M

2

A B C D E F G H I J K L M

*Work short
stitches over
two threads*

1 Start at top left. Work five upright stitches in a diamond shape from **7B** to **5B**, **8C** to **4C**, **9D** to **3D**, **8E** to **4E** and **7F** to **5F**. Repeat to the end of the line, leaving one space between each diamond.

2 Work a zigzag line above and below the diamonds. Start at **4A** to **6A**, then work three stitches upward from **3B** to **5B**, **2C** to **4C** and **1D** to **3D**, and two downward from **2E** to **4E** and **3F** to **5F**. Repeat to the end of the row, then work a mirror image below, starting at **8M** to **6M**. Continue working alternate rows of diamonds and chevrons to fill the required area.

Diamond

1

Work diamonds
in blocks
of five stitches

Work each line of
diamonds into spaces
below previous row

2

Stitch second
row in opposite
direction

········· LEVEL ·········
Easy

·········· USES ··········
Fillings and backgrounds

········· METHOD ·········
*Large-scale variation of
Hungarian stitch*

········· MATERIALS ·········
*Single canvas; any thread
in one or two colors*

1 Start at top left. Work five upright stitches from **5A** to **3A**, **6B** to **2B**, **7C** to **1C**, **6D** to **2D** and **5E** to **3E**. Repeat to the end of the line, leaving one space between each block.

2 The second row is worked from right to left, using the same or a different color. Start the first block at **8N** to **6N**, then repeat these two rows to continue.

Long Stitch Triangles

Work eight
upright stitches
to form first
triangle

1

Make longest stitches
below shortest stitches of
previous row

2

Stitch second row
from right to left

········· LEVEL ·········
Easy

·········· USES ··········
*Textured single-color
background or filling*

········· METHOD ·········
*Two rows of interlocking
straight stitch triangles,
repeated horizontally*

········· MATERIALS ·········
Single canvas; any thread

1 Start in the top left corner with five progressively longer stitches, worked from **2A** to **1A**, **3B** to **1B**, **4C** to **1C**, **5D** to **1D** and **6E** to **1E**. Work three shorter stitches from **5F** to **1F**, **4G** to **1G** and **3H** to **1H**. Repeat this block to the end of the line.

2 Make a long stitch from **7Q** to **2Q**, then work four shorter stitches from **7P** to **3P**, **7O** to **4O**, **7N** to **5N** and **7M** to **6M**, and three longer stitches from **7L** to **5L**, **7K** to **4K** and **7J** to **3J**. Repeat these two rows to fill the required area.

Lozenge

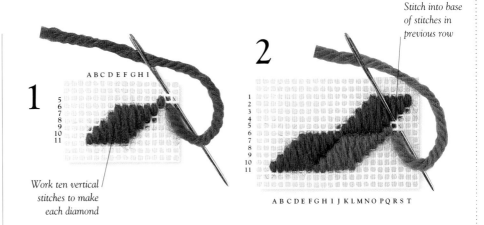

2 *Stitch into base of stitches in previous row*

Work ten vertical stitches to make each diamond

LEVEL
Intermediate

USES
Harlequin filling or background for large areas

METHOD
Elongated diamonds, worked in interlocking diagonal rows

MATERIALS
Single canvas; two colors of any thread

1 Start at bottom left with five stitches from **11A** to **10A**, **11B** to **9B**, **11C** to **8C**, **11D** to **7D** and **11E** to **6E**. Complete the diamond with five more stitches from **11F** to **6F**, **10G** to **6G**, **9H** to **6H**, **8I** to **6I** and **7J** to **6J**. Begin the next diamond at **6K** to **5K** and contine working upward.

2 Using a different color, begin the second row at **11G** to **10G**. Work the third row in the first color, starting at **11M** to **10M**. Fill in the required space above the stitches with further rows in alternate colors.

Straight Milanese

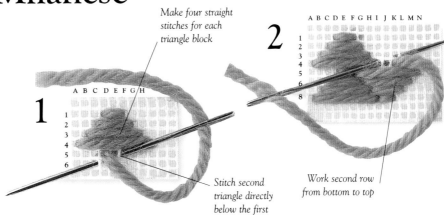

Make four straight stitches for each triangle block

2

Stitch second triangle directly below the first

Work second row from bottom to top

LEVEL
Intermediate

USES
Background or filling

METHOD
Interlocking rows of triangles worked vertically to create a wave pattern

MATERIALS
Single canvas; any thread in one or two colors

1 Start at top left. Work four horizontal stitches from **1D** to **1F**, **2C** to **2G**, **3B** to **3H** and **4A** to **4I**. Begin the next triangle at **5D** to **5F** and continue downward to the end of the row.

2 Begin the next row with four stitches from **8K** to **8I**, **7L** to **7H**, **6M** to **6G** and **5N** to **5F**. Continue working upward, then repeat these two rows to fill the required area.

TECHNIQUE VARIATION

For a more geometric effect, work alternate rows in contrasting or toning colors, to emphasize the triangular formation of straight milanese stitch.

Double Brick

···· OTHER NAME ····
Double Gobelin filling

········ LEVEL ········
Easy

········ USES ········
Single color filling

······ METHOD ······
*Interlocking rows of
double straight stitches*

······ MATERIALS ······
Single canvas; any thread

1

*Work each
upright stitch
over four threads*

2

*Stitch second row
from right to left*

1 Start at top left. Work two parallel stitches from **5A** to **1A** and **5B** to **1B**, then two more from **7C** to **3C** and **7D** to **3D**. Come up at **5E** and continue working pairs of staggered straight stitches to the end of the row.

2 Work the second and subsequent rows in the same way, starting with a pair of stitches from **9J** to **5J** and **9I** to **5I**.

Brick Filling

*Work each
horizontal stitch
over four threads*

1

*Work each upright
stitch over one thread*

2

*Avoid catching long
stitches with needle*

········ LEVEL ········
Intermediate

········ USES ········
Small-scale fillings

······ METHOD ······
*Pairs of horizontal
straight stitches divided by
vertical stitches*

······ MATERIALS ······
*Single canvas; any thread
in two colors*

1 Starting at bottom left, work two horizontal stitches from **10G** to **10C** and **9G** to **9C**, then a second staggered pair from **8E** to **8A** and **7E** to **7A**. Continue upward, then work the second row downward in the same way, starting at **1K** to **1G**. Repeat these two rows to fill the required area.

2 Using a contrasting thread, work short upright stitches at the points where pairs of stitches meet, starting with **1G** to **2G**.

······ TECHNIQUE VARIATION ·······

Working the vertical stitches (see step 2, above) in the same thread as the horizontal stitches produces a more textured surface with a quilted appearance.

Long and Short Brick

···· OTHER NAME ·····
Brick stitch

········· LEVEL ·········
Intermediate

··········· USES ···········
Fillings and backgrounds

········ METHOD ········
*Alternate pairs of long
and short stitches*

····· MATERIALS ·····
*Single canvas; one or two
colors of any thread*

*Leave two spaces between
each pair of straight stitches*

*Work each long
stitch over six
horizontal threads*

*Use a contrasting
thread for
short stitches*

*Stitch into
same holes as
previous
stitches*

1 Start at top left and work two stitches from **7A** to
1A and **7B** to **1B**. Make two more from **7E** to **1E** and
7F to **1F**. Repeat to the end of the row, leaving two
spaces between each pair of stitches. Start the next
row with **11H** to **5H** and **11G** to **5G** and continue
working from right to left.

2 Fill in the spaces with pairs of short stitches,
starting with **5C** to **3C** and **5D** to **3D**. Repeat these
two steps to continue.

Basket Filling

········· LEVEL ·········
Intermediate

··········· USES ···········
*Large-scale woven-look
filling or background*

········ METHOD ········
*Straight stitch worked in
alternate vertical and
horizontal blocks*

····· MATERIALS ·····
Single canvas; any thread

*Slip needle
under vertical
stitch before
inserting*

*Work each stitch
over six threads*

1 Start at top left. Work a block of five upright stitches
from **7B** to **1B**, **7C** to **1C**, **7D** to **1D**, **7E** to **1E** and **7F**
to **1F**; then work a block of five horizontal stitches from
2L to **2F**, **3L** to **3F**, **4L** to **4F**, **5L** to **5F** and **6L** to **6F**.
Repeat to the end of the line.

2 Work five upright stitches below the horizontal block,
starting with **12K** to **6K** and ending with **12G** to **6G**.
Work a horizontal block under the upright block starting
at **7A** to **7F** and ending with **12A** to **12F**. Repeat to the
end of the line, then repeat these two rows to continue.

Diagonal Needlepoint Stitches

THIS SECTION STARTS with tent stitch and its variations, which are the most frequently used needlepoint stitches. Like all the other diagonal stitches, they are worked at a slant across the thread intersections. This can have the effect of distorting the square weave of the canvas, even when it is mounted in a frame. The finished piece should be stretched and blocked back into shape. Some diagonal stitches are worked on single canvas, others on double. Always match the thickness of the thread or yarn to the weight of the canvas being used, so that no background threads are visible.

Half Cross

········ LEVEL ········
Easy

·········· USES ··········
Charts; printed canvases

········ METHOD ········
Small slanting stitches

······ MATERIALS ······
Double canvas; thick yarn

········· TIP ··········
Turn work upside down for return journey to stitch rows in same direction.

Start at top left. Stitch over one intersection, from **2A** to **1B** and **2B** to **1C**, then repeat to the end of the line. Begin the next row with **2F** to **3E** and **2E** to **3D**. Repeat these two rows to continue.

Basketweave Tent

···· OTHER NAMES ·····
Continental stitch; diagonal tent stitch

········· LEVEL ·········
Intermediate

·········· USES ··········
Backgrounds and fillings

········ METHOD ········
Tent stitch worked in diagonal rows

······ MATERIALS ······
Single canvas; any thread

Starting at top right, make a stitch from **2E** to **1F**. Work the next row upward from **3E** to **2F** and **2D** to **1E** and the third downward from **2C** to **1D**, **3D** to **2E** and **4E** to **3F**. Begin the following row with **5E** to **4F**: continue working up, then down.

Tent

····· OTHER NAME ·····
Petit point

········· LEVEL ·········
Easy

·········· USES ··········
Backgrounds; detailed charted or printed patterns

········ METHOD ········
Worked horizontally

······ MATERIALS ······
Single canvas; any thread

Take needle behind two threads to make long stitch on reverse side

1 Start at top right and sew a diagonal stitch from **2F** to **1G**. Work the second stitch from **2E** to **1F** and repeat to the end of the row.

2 Turn the canvas the other way up and repeat step 1, or work the second row from left to right, starting with **2B** to **3A**. Repeat these two rows.

Work each stitch in same direction

Keep needle at an angle

·················· STITCH VARIATION··················

Trammed tent stitch is sewn over long straight stitches worked through the small holes on a double canvas. This gives a ridged effect and because it is hardwearing, this stitch is often used for seat covers.

Gobelin

····· OTHER NAMES ·····
Oblique Gobelin;
gros point

········ LEVEL ········
Easy

··········· USES ···········
Backgrounds and fillings

········ METHOD ········
Long diagonal stitches
worked in horizontal rows

······ MATERIALS ······
Single canvas, any thread

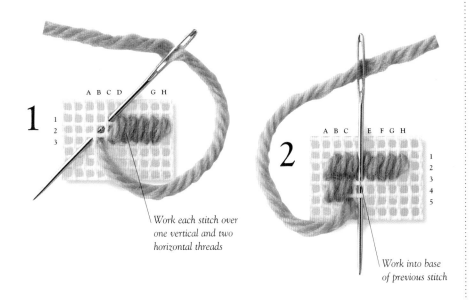

Work each stitch over
one vertical and two
horizontal threads

Work into base
of previous stitch

1 Start at top right. Make the first diagonal stitch from **3G** to **1H** and the next from **3F** to **1G**. Repeat to the end of the line.

2 Begin the return journey with two stitches from **5A** to **3B** and **5B** to **3C**, and continue to the end of the row. Repeat these two rows to fill the required area.

Encroaching Gobelin

········ LEVEL ········
Easy

··········· USES ···········
Backgrounds; filling for
plain or shaded areas

········ METHOD ········
Overlapping rows of
diagonal stitches, worked
horizontally

······ MATERIALS ······
Single canvas; any yarn

Work over five
horizontal threads
to fill larger areas

Stitch over one
vertical and three
horizontal threads

Work second row so
stitches overlap first
row by one thread

1 Starting at top right, work a row of diagonal stitches, beginning with **4F** to **1G** and **4E** to **1F**.

2 Work the first stitch of the next row from **6A** to **3B** and the second from **6B** to **3C**. Continue to the end of the line and repeat these two steps to continue.

Reversed Sloping Gobelin

········ LEVEL ········
Easy

········· USES ·········
*Plain or shaded fillings
and backgrounds*

········ METHOD ········
*Vertical rows of diagonal
straight stitches worked
alternately down and up*

······· MATERIALS ·······
Any canvas; any thread

*Make stitch
over two thread
intersections*

1 Start at top left and work a diagonal stitch from **3C** to **1A**. Work the next stitch from **4C** to **2A** and repeat downward to the end of the line.

2 Begin the next line with a stitch in the opposite direction from **6E** to **8C**, then continue working upward. Repeat these two rows.

*Work second
row at right
angles to first*

········ TECHNIQUE VARIATION ········
To produce a shaded effect, work the stitches in the lower part of the stitched area with a selection of progressively darker tones of the main color.

Canvas Stem

········ LEVEL ········
Intermediate

········· USES ·········
*Textured background,
filling or chevron border*

········ METHOD ········
*Two upright rows of
diagonal stitches, set in a
V-shape, and divided by
lines of back stitch*

······· MATERIALS ·······
*Double canvas; two
colors of any yarn*

*Work each
stitch over
three thread
intersections*

*Ensure back stitches
conceal horizontal
threads*

*Use contrasting
thread for back
stitch*

1 Starting at top left, make a diagonal stitch from **4D** to **1A**. Work the second stitch directly below, from **5D** to **2A**, and continue stitching downward. Begin the next row at **6G** to **9D**. Make another stitch from **5G** to **8D** and continue working upward. Repeat these two rows to cover the required area.

2 Make two back stitches from **4D** to **3D** and **5D** to **4D** and continue downward. Work further rows of back stitch into the holes between the lines of diagonal stitches.

Florence

····· OTHER NAME ·····
Diagonal mosaic stitch

········· LEVEL ·········
Easy

··········· USES ···········
Plain or striped fillings

········· METHOD ·········
*Alternate long and short
slanting stitches, worked
diagonally*

······· MATERIALS ·······
Any canvas; any thread

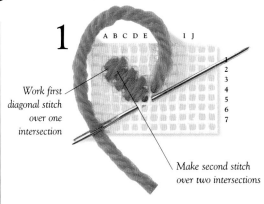

Work first diagonal stitch over one intersection

Make second stitch over two intersections

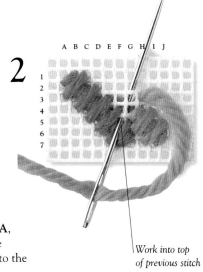

Work into top of previous stitch

1 Start at top left. Make a short stitch from **1B** to **2A**, followed by a longer stitch from **1C** to **3A**. Continue working alternate long and short stitches downward to the bottom edge of the area being filled.

2 The next row is worked upward using the same or a different color yarn. Begin with a short stitch from **6J** to **7I** and a long one from **5J** to **7H** and repeat to the end of the row. Repeat these two steps to continue.

Cashmere

········· LEVEL ·········
Easy

··········· USES ···········
*Textured plain or striped
backgrounds and fillings*

········· METHOD ·········
*Groups of three diagonal
stitches worked vertically*

······· MATERIALS ·······
Any canvas; any thread

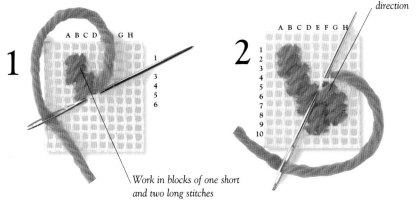

Work in blocks of one short and two long stitches

Stitch second row in opposite direction

1 Starting at top left, make a short diagonal stitch from **1B** to **2A**. Work two longer stitches from **1C** to **3A** and **2C** to **4A**. Repeat these three stitches, working downward to the end of the row.

2 The next row is worked upward. Make a short stitch from **8H** to **9G** and the next two long stitches from **7H** to **9F** and **6H** to **8F**. Repeat steps 1 and 2 to fill the required area.

······· TECHNIQUE VARIATION ·······

Work alternate rows in a second color to create a pattern of ridged diagonal stripes.

Diagonal

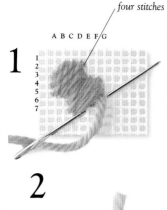

Work in blocks of four stitches

A B C D E F G

1

1
2
3
4
5
6
7

2

A B C D E F G H I J K

1
2
3
4
5
6
7
8
9
10
11
12

15

Work the second row in the same or a contrasting color

········ LEVEL ········
Easy

········· USES ·········
Plain or striped filling or background for large areas

········ METHOD ········
Graduated straight stitches worked in diagonal rows

······ MATERIALS ······
Any canvas; one or two colors of any thread

1 Start at the top left corner. Each row is made up of blocks of four stitches, beginning with **1C** to **3A**, **1D** to **4A**, **1E** to **5A** and **2E** to **5B**. Work the first stitch of the next block from **3E** to **5C** and continue working downward.

2 The next row is worked upward in the same way. Make the first block from **13I** to **15G**, **12I** to **15F**, **11I** to **15E** and **11H** to **14E**. Repeat these two rows to continue and fill in the spaces with additonal diagonal stitches (see p.19).

············ TECHNIQUE VARIATION ············

For a more unusual effect, use one color to sew the diagonal stitch, then work rows of contrasting back stitch (see p.40) between the lines. This will conceal any canvas that may show through and creates the illusion of a set of diagonal laid threads couched by zigzag lines of back stitch.

Byzantine

1

1
2
4
5
6
7

B C D E F G

2

A B C D E F G H I J K L M

1
2
3
4
5
6
7
8
9
10

······ OTHER NAME ······
Step stitch

········ LEVEL ········
Easy

········· USES ·········
Large scale fillings and backgrounds

········ METHOD ········
Diagonal straight stitches, worked in zigzag lines

······ MATERIALS ······
Any canvas; any thread

3

A B C D E F G H I J K L M N O P

1
2
3
4
5
6
7
8
9
10
11
12
13
14
15

1 Start at top left. Each zigzag is made up of repeated blocks of six diagonal stitches. Work the first four stitches downward from **1D** to **4A**, **2D** to **5A**, **3D** to **6A** and **4D** to **7A**. The next two stitches are worked to the right, from **4E** to **7B** and **4F** to **7C**. Start the next block at **4G**.

2 Work the second row level with and to the right of the first, starting at **1J** to **4G**. Make further rows to the right to fill the area required.

3 Complete any space at the bottom left corner with extra zigzags, starting at **10A** to **7D**, then work short stitches to fill the gaps (see p.19).

Jacquard

1

*Make eight
stitches for
each block*

2

*Work each diagonal
stitch over two
intersections*

*Work tent stitch
over one intersection*

3

4

*Fill in
unworked
canvas with
part stitches*

1 Start at top left. Work a block of five diagonal stitches downward from **3D** to **1F**, **4D** to **2F**, **5D** to **3F**, **6D** to **4F** and **7D** to **5F**, and three to the right from **7E** to **5G**, **7F** to **5H** and **7G** to **5I**.

2 Repeat this block to the bottom right corner of the area to be filled.

3 Using the second color, work a block of five tent stitches downward from **4C** to **3D**, **5C** to **4D**, and **6C** to **5D**, **7C** to **6D** and **8C** to **7D** and three to the right from **8D** to **7E**, **8E** to **7F**, **8F** to **7G**. Repeat this block to the end of the row.

4 Repeat step 1, starting with **6A** to **4C**, then continue working these two rows in alternate colors to fill the space.

Moorish

········· LEVEL ·········
Intermediate

········· USES ·········
*Large-scale filling with
zigzag pattern*

········· METHOD ·········
*Alternate rows of
graduated diagonal
stitches and tent stitch*

········· MATERIALS ·········
*Any canvas; any thread
in one or two colors*

1

*Work diagonal
stitches to form row
of square blocks*

2

*Make tent
stitch over one
intersection*

1 Start at top left. Work three diagonal stitches which increase in length from **2B** to **1C**, **3B** to **1D** and **4A** to **1E**, then a shorter stitch from **4C** to **2E**. Repeat these four stitches to continue the row.

2 Using the second thread, work a stepped line of tent stitch to the left of the first row. Start with **2B** to **3A**, **3B** to **4A**, **4B** to **5A** and **4C** to **5B**, then repeat these four stitches. Repeat steps 1 and 2 to continue, working each successive row into the spaces left by the row before.

Milanese

········· LEVEL ·········
Intermediate

········· USES ·········
*Brocade-like background
or filling for larger areas*

········· METHOD ·········
*Diagonal rows of
alternate long and short
back stitch forming
triangular pattern*

········· MATERIALS ·········
Any canvas; any thread

1

*Work the first
row downward*

2

*Make stitches
over three,
then two
interstections*

3

1 Start at top right. Work a long stitch from **5G** to **1K** and a short stitch from **6F** to **5G**, then repeat these two stitches to the end of the line. Start the next row with a short stitch from **10C** to **12A** and a long stitch from **7F** to **10C**, and repeat these two stitches, working upward.

2 Start the third row with **5I** to **3K** and **8F** to **5I**, and repeat these two stitches, working downward.

3 Work the fourth row upward, starting with **10E** to **14A** and **9F** to **10E**. Repeat these four rows to continue.

Mosaic

········ LEVEL ········
Easy

·········· USES ··········
Fine textured backgrounds

········ METHOD ········
Long and short diagonal stitches worked in horizontal rows to form square pattern

········ MATERIALS ········
Any canvas, any thread

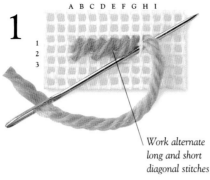

Work alternate long and short diagonal stitches

Fill in spaces with short stitches

1 Start at top left with two diagonal stitches from **1B** to **2A** and **1C** to **3A**. Repeat these two stitches to the end of the line.

2 Work the second row in the opposite direction. Make a short stitch from **3H** to **2I** to complete the first square, then continue working toward the left. Repeat these two rows to fill the required area.

········ TECHNIQUE VARIATION ········
Change the visual effect by working the squares in two or more toning or contrasting colors to make a checkered pattern, ideal for filling smaller areas.

Cushion

········ LEVEL ········
Easy

·········· USES ··········
Filling or background with regular pattern of squares

········ METHOD ········
Graduated diagonal stitches worked in squares

········ MATERIALS ········
Any canvas; any thread

Work diagonal stitches to form a square block

1 Starting at the top left corner, work five stitches from **1B** to **2A**, **1C** to **3A**, **1D** to **4A**, **2D** to **4B** and **3D** to **4C**. Start the next block at **1E** to **2D** and continue to the end of the row.

2 Work the second row in the opposite direction, starting at **5G** to **4H**. Repeat steps 1 and 2 until the required space is filled.

········ TECHNIQUE VARIATION ········

To prevent the canvas distorting, the square blocks can be worked in alternate directions using one or two colors.

Scottish

········ LEVEL ········

Intermediate

········ USES ········

Filling for large areas

········ METHOD ········

*Cushion stitches framed
with a line of tent stitch*

········ MATERIALS ········

Any canvas; any thread

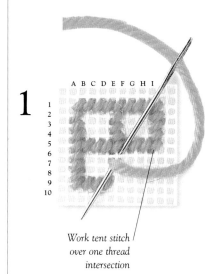

1

*Work tent stitch
over one thread
intersection*

*Make five diagonal
stitches to fill square*

2

1 Starting at top left, work the tent stitch frame
(see p.129). Make a grid of horizontal and vertical
rows, leaving a square of three canvas threads
between the lines.

2 Fill the squares with cushion stitch (see p.136),
using a second color. Work the first block from **2C**
to **3B**, **2D** to **4B**, **2E** to **5B**, **3E** to **5C** and **4E** to
5D, then come up at **2G** to start the next square.

Checker

········ LEVEL ········

Intermediate

········ USES ········

Textured fillings

········ METHOD ········

*Alternate large
cushion stitches and
square tent stitch blocks*

········ MATERIALS ········

*Any canvas; any thread
in one or two colors*

1

*Leave four
threads
between each
cushion stitch*

*Fill in spaces with
squares of tent stitch*

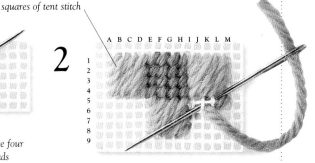

2

1 Start at top left with the first cushion stitch. Make seven
diagonal stitches from **1B** to **2A**, **1C** to **3A**, **1D** to **4A**, **1E** to
5A, **2E** to **5B**, **3E** to **5C** and **4E** to **5D**. Begin the next block
with **1J** to **2I** and start the next row at **6E** to **5F**.

2 Using a second color, work squares of tent stitch (see p.139)
in the spaces between the cushion stitches. Starting with **2H** to
1I, work four stitches, then work another three rows directly
below. Repeat to fill all the unworked squares.

Cross and Star Needlepoint Stitches

THIS SECTION INCLUDES all the stitches that are worked with a combination of horizontal, vertical, and diagonal stitches. The various cross stitches feature two or more straight stitches that cross over each other, while the individual stitches that make up the star stitches radiate from a central point. The heavier cross variations are all worked on double canvas to give better coverage; the other stitches use single canvas. Whichever background is being used, the chosen thread should be thick enough to cover the canvas completely. This group of stitches should all be worked in a frame.

Cross

Work each diagonal stitch over one intersection

····· OTHER NAME ·····
Berlin stitch

··········· LEVEL ···········
Easy

··········· USES ···········
Charted and printed designs; backgrounds

········ METHOD ········
Individual cross stitches, worked horizontally

········ MATERIALS ········
Double canvas; any thread or yarn

Start at top right with two stitches from **1E** to **2D** and **1D** to **2E**. Begin the next cross at **1D** to **2C** and continue to the left. Work the first cross of the next row at **3A** to **2B** and **3B** to **2A**, then continue to the right. Repeat these two rows.

Diagonal Cross

Stitch over two intersections

··········· LEVEL ···········
Easy

··········· USES ···········
Backgrounds and fillings

········ METHOD ········
Single cross stitches, worked in diagonal rows

········ MATERIALS ········
Single canvas; any thread

Start at bottom left. Work three crosses from **5A** to **7C** and **5C** to **7A**; **7E** to **5C** and **7C** to **5E**; **5C** to **3A** and **5A** to **3C**. Begin the next row at **1A** to **3C** and **1C** to **3A**, and start the second cross at **3C** to **5E**. Repeat these two rows.

Double Cross

Work each cross over one thread intersection

Make crosses below spaces in previous row

Work second stitch of each cross in same direction

··········· LEVEL ···········
Intermediate

··········· USES ···········
Two-colored backgrounds

········ METHOD ········
Spaced cross stitches with overlapping rows of elongated crosses

······ MATERIALS ······
Double canvas; thin and thick thread in two colors

1 Start at top right, using the fine thread. Make two crosses from **2H** to **3G** and **2G** to **3H**, then **2F** to **3E** and **2E** to **3F** and continue toward the left. Begin the next row with **4C** to **5B** and **4B** to **5C** and **4E** to **5D** and **4D** to **5E**. Repeat these two rows.

2 Fill in the spaces with rows of long crosses in the thick thread, worked in alternate directions. Start with **4F** to **1G** and **4G** to **1F** and work toward the left. Begin the next row with a cross from **6A** to **3B** and **6B** to **3A** and continue toward the right.

Upright Cross

···· OTHER NAME ····
Straight cross

········ LEVEL ········
Easy

········· USES ·········
Fine textured backgrounds

······· METHOD ·······
*Crosses worked singly in
interlocking diagonal rows*

······ MATERIALS ······
Any canvas; any thread

Start at top left with two
crosses from **3B** to **1B** and
2A to **2C**, and **4C** to **2C**
and **3B** to **3D**; continue
downward. Start the next
row with **7D** to **5D** and **6C**
to **6E**, **6C** to **4C** and **5B** to
5D and continue upward.
Repeat these two rows to
fill the required area.

Diamond Cross

········ LEVEL ········
Intermediate

········· USES ·········
*Raised backgrounds and
textured fillings*

······· METHOD ·······
*Cross stitches worked over
larger upright cross stitches*

······ MATERIALS ······
Single canvas; any thread

*Make sure
diagonal stitches
lie in same
direction*

Start at top left. Work an
upright cross from **3E** to **3A**
and **5C** to **1C** covered by a
cross from **4D** to **2B** and **4B**
to **2D**. Begin the next stitch
at **5G** to **5C**, then continue
working in diagonal rows.

Smyrna Cross

*Work stitch over
five thread
intersections*

*Always work
stitches in
same order*

···· OTHER NAME ····
Leviathan stitch

········ LEVEL ········
Easy

········· USES ·········
Raised backgrounds

······· METHOD ·······
*Upright cross worked over
cross stitch*

······ MATERIALS ······
Single canvas; any thread

1 Start at top left with a diagonal stitch from
1A to **5E** crossed by a second stitch from **5A**
to **1E**. Bring the needle out at **5C**.

2 Make an upright stitch to **1C** and a
horizontal stitch from **3A** to **3E**. Bring the
needle out at **1E** to begin the next stitch,
then continue working in horizontal rows.

······· TECHNIQUE VARIATION ·······

Work alternate crosses in
toning or contrasting
colors to create an
all-over checker pattern,
for a colorful background.

Double Leviathan

········ LEVEL ········
Intermediate

········· USES ·········
Highly textured filling

········ METHOD ········
Smyrna cross variation

······ MATERIALS ······
Single canvas; any yarn or thread – lustrous pearl cotton gives good result

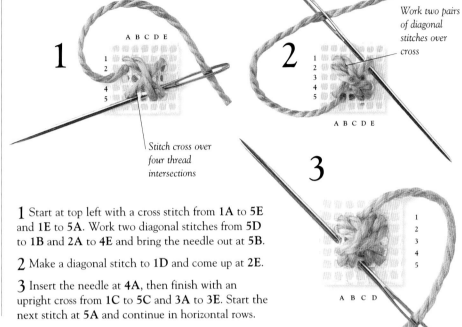

1

Stitch cross over four thread intersections

2 Work two pairs of diagonal stitches over cross

3

1 Start at top left with a cross stitch from **1A** to **5E** and **1E** to **5A**. Work two diagonal stitches from **5D** to **1B** and **2A** to **4E** and bring the needle out at **5B**.

2 Make a diagonal stitch to **1D** and come up at **2E**.

3 Insert the needle at **4A**, then finish with an upright cross from **1C** to **5C** and **3A** to **3E**. Start the next stitch at **5A** and continue in horizontal rows.

Diagonal Tweed

········· LEVEL ·········
Intermediate

·········· USES ··········
Two-color filling with raised surface

········ METHOD ········
Smyrna crosses alternated with large crosses covered by small upright crosses

······ MATERIALS ······
Single canvas; two colors of any thread

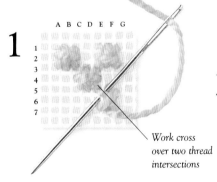

1

Work cross over two thread intersections

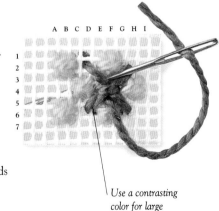

2

Use a contrasting color for large double crosses

1 Starting at top left, work a series of small Smyrna cross stitches (see left). Leave two threads between each stitch and work the crosses in subsequent rows beneath these gaps.

2 Using the second thread, work a cross stitch from **6H** to **2D** and **6D** to **2H**. Make a horizontal stitch from **4E** to **4G**, then an upright stitch from **6F** to **3F**. Start the next large cross at **6D** and repeat along the row.

Broad Cross

·········· LEVEL ··········
Intermediate

··········· USES ···········
*Basketweave filling for
large areas*

········· METHOD ·········
*Large square crosses
worked in horizontal rows*

······· MATERIALS ·······
Single canvas; any thread

*Work straight
stitches over
six thread
intersections*

*Insert needle
into base of
previous row*

1 Start at top left. Work a block of three upright stitches from **7C** to **1C**, **7D** to **1D** and **7E** to **1E**, crossed by three horizontal stitches from **5A** to **5G**, **4A** to **4G** and **3A** to **3G**. Begin the next block at **7I** to **1I** and continue to the end of the row.

2 The second row fits into the spaces between the crosses; begin the first block at **11F** and work subsequent rows in the same way, alternately from right to left.

Cross-corner Cushion

·········· LEVEL ··········
Intermediate

··········· USES ···········
Filling for large areas

········· METHOD ·········
*Cushion stitch variation
with two layers of stitches,
forming a diagonal pattern*

······· MATERIALS ·······
*Single canvas; any thread
– twisted embroidery
cotton gives good results*

*Work square
over five thread
intersections*

*Work second
layer of stitches
at right angles
to first*

1 Start at top left with a square of nine graduated diagonal stitches starting at **2F** to **1E** and ending with **6B** to **5A**.

2 Work five more stitches in the opposite direction, from **1F** to **6A**, **2F** to **6B**, **3F** to **6C**, **4F** to **6D** and **5F** to **6E**.

3 Repeat steps 1 and 2 along the row, reversing every other square. Work the next and subsequent rows as a mirror image of the one above.

Brighton

········· LEVEL ·········
Intermediate

·········· USES ··········
*Dense fillings and
backgrounds*

········ METHOD ········
*Straight stitch hexagons,
interspersed with
contrasting upright crosses*

······· MATERIALS ·······
*Single canvas; two
colors of any thread*

*Alternate direction
of diagonal stitches
for each block*

*Work upright cross
in space between
diagonal stitches*

1 Starting at top left, make a hexagonal block of five diagonal stitches from **1C** to **3A**, **1D** to **4A**, **1E** to **5A**, **2E** to **5B** and **3E** to **5C**.

2 Reverse the direction for the second hexagon, starting at **3I** to **1G**. Repeat these two blocks to the end of the line. Work each subsequent row as a mirror image of the one above.

3 Using a contrasting thread, work an upright cross from **4E** to **6E** and **5D** to **5F**. Repeat to fill each space.

Rice

····· OTHER NAME ·····
William and Mary stitch

········ LEVEL ········
Intermediate

·········· USES ··········
Solid lattice filling

········ METHOD ········
*Back stitch square worked
over large cross stitch*

······· MATERIALS ·······
*Single canvas; one thick
and one fine thread*

*Make each
cross over five
intersections*

*Work back stitch
in contrasting
color*

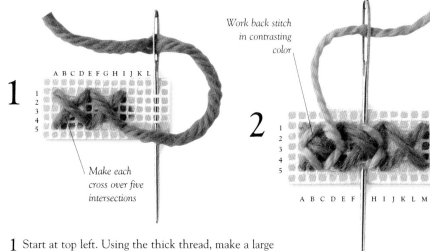

1 Start at top left. Using the thick thread, make a large cross stitch from **5A** to **1E** and **5E** to **1A**. Begin the next cross at **5E** to **1I** and continue along the row.

2 With the fine thread, work four back stitches over the first cross from **3E** to **5C**, **1C** to **3E**, **3A** to **1C** and **5C** to **3A**. Repeat for each cross, starting the next back stitch square at **3I** to **5G**. Work the following rows in the same way, directly below the first.

Plaited Gobelin

.... LEVEL ....
Easy

.... USES ....
*Woven effect backgrounds;
filling for large areas*

.... METHOD ....
*Gobelin variation, worked
in overlapping rows*

.... MATERIALS ....
*Double canvas; tapestry
yarn or other thick thread*

*Insert needle into
space between
stitches*

*Work in overlapping
rows to produce
plaited effect*

1 Start at the top right corner with a diagonal stitch from **3E** to **1D**. Work the next from **3D** to **1C** and continue stitching toward the left.

2 Begin the next row at **4A** to **2B** and repeat this stitch to the end of the row.

3 Work the third row as the first, starting at **5E** to **3D**. Continue working alternately to the left, then right.

Greek

.... LEVEL ....
Easy

.... USES ....
*In single rows as outline;
textured filling*

.... METHOD ....
*Herringbone variation,
worked in horizontal rows*

.... MATERIALS ....
*Double canvas; any
thick thread*

*Work alternate
long and short
diagonal stitches*

1 Start at top left. Make a short stitch from **1C** to **3A**, then a long stitch from **1A** to **3E**. Come up at **3C**.

2 Make a short stitch to **1E,** then continue working alternate long and short stitches to the end of the line.

3 Work the second row in the opposite direction starting with **5G** to **3E** and **3G** to **5C**. Repeat these two rows to continue.

Plait

········· LEVEL ·········
Easy

·········· USES ··········
*Solid ridged backgrounds,
in single row as outline*

········· METHOD ·········
*Rows of overlapping
straight stitches*

······· MATERIALS ·······
*Double canvas;
any thick thread*

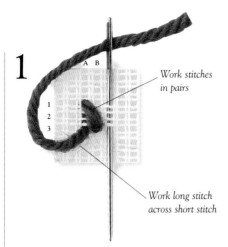

1

Work stitches
in pairs

Work long stitch
across short stitch

2

Come up at base
of first stitch

1 Start at top left with a diagonal stitch from **3B** to **1A**, crossed by a longer stitch from **3A** to **1C**. Come out at **3C** to start the next pair of stitches.

2 Work a short stitch up to **1B** and come out at **3B**. Continue working pairs of stitches to the end of the line; then stitch the second and subsequent rows directly below the first.

····· TECHNIQUE VARIATION ·····

Plait stitch can also be worked in vertical rows, depending on the effect required and the shape of the area to be filled.

Fishbone

········· LEVEL ·········
Intermediate

·········· USES ··········
*Textured chevron filling
for large areas*

········· METHOD ·········
*Diagonal stitches worked
in alternate directions in
vertical rows*

······· MATERIALS ·······
*Double canvas; tapestry
yarn or other thick thread*

Work first row
upward

1

Work short stitch across
top of long stitch

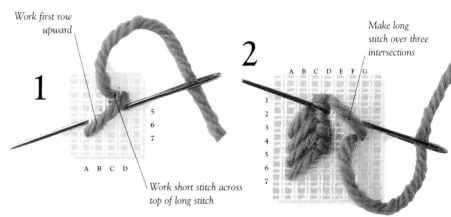

2

Make long
stitch over three
intersections

1 Start at bottom left. Make a long diagonal stitch from **7A** to **4D** and a short stitch from **4C** to **5D**. Come up at **6A** and repeat these two stitches to the end of the row.

2 Work the second row downward. Make the first two stitches from **1D** to **4G** and **4F** to **3G**, then come up at **2D**. Repeat steps 1 and 2 to fill the required area.

····· TECHNIQUE VARIATION ·····

Repeat step 1 only to vary the surface of the stitch and work the rows in alternate light and dark colors to make a pattern of bold ridged vertical stripes.

Fern

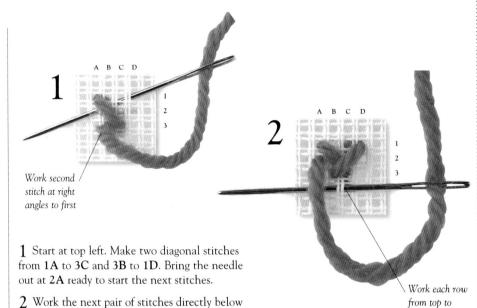

1

Work second stitch at right angles to first

2

Work each row from top to bottom

········ LEVEL ········
Easy

·········· USES ··········
Ridged fillings and backgrounds

········ METHOD ········
Pairs of overlapping diagonal stitches worked in vertical rows

······· MATERIALS ·······
Double canvas; any thick thread or yarn

1 Start at top left. Make two diagonal stitches from **1A** to **3C** and **3B** to **1D**. Bring the needle out at **2A** ready to start the next stitches.

2 Work the next pair of stitches directly below the first, from **2A** to **4C** and **4B** to **2D**. Continue working downward to the end of the row. Start the next row at **1D**.

Fir

1

Work second side as mirror image of first

2

Make eleven straight stitches for each block

····· OTHER NAME ·····
Leaf stitch

·········· LEVEL ··········
Intermediate

·········· USES ··········
Filling for large areas

········ METHOD ········
Interlocking rows of hexagonal blocks

······· MATERIALS ·······
Any canvas; any thread

1 Start at top left with an upright stitch from **1D** to **5D**. Work three slanting stitches from **2C** to **5D**, **3B** to **6D** and **4A** to **7D**. Make two more stitches directly below, from **5A** to **8D** and **7A** to **9D**. Come up at **2E**.

2 Make six stitches to mirror step 1 from **2E** to **5D**, to **7G** to **9D**. Start the second block with **1J** to **5J** and continue working to the right. Stitch the next row into the spaces below the first.

········ TECHNIQUE VARIATION ········

Work an upright stitch from 5D to 9D to vary the leaf shape and stitch the rows in two contrasting colors to create a striped filling.

Rhodes

········ LEVEL ········
Intermediate

········· USES ·········
3-dimensional fillings or background

········ METHOD ········
Raised square stitch worked in straight rows

······ MATERIALS ······
Single canvas; any thread

Work stitches counter-clockwise

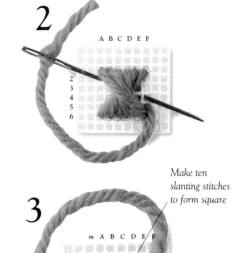

Make ten slanting stitches to form square

Make sure each block is worked in same order

1 Start at top left and work four diagonal stitches from **6A** to **1F**, **6B** to **1E**, **6C** to **1D** and **6D** to **1C**. Come up at **6E**.

2 Work another two stitches from **6E** to **1B**, and **6F** to **1A**. Insert the needle at **1B**, then come up at **4F**.

3 Make three more stitches to complete the square from **4F** to **3A**, **3F** to **4A** and **2F** to **5A**. Come up at **6F**, ready to make the next block. Work the following rows directly below.

Half Rhodes

········ LEVEL ········
Intermediate

········· USES ·········
Striped raised filling for large areas or backgrounds

········ METHOD ········
Rhodes stitch variation worked in diagonal rows

······ MATERIALS ······
Single canvas; any thread in one or two colors

Stitch each block in same direction

Work the second row into the spaces below the first

1 Start at top left. Make five overlapping straight stitches from **5A** to **1E**, **5B** to **1D**, **5C** to **1C**, **5D** to **1B** and **5E** to **1A**. Come up at **7D** to make the next block, then continue working downward to the right.

2 Stitch the second row in a different color, starting at **9A** to **5E**. Work the next and subsequent rows directly below the first.

Star

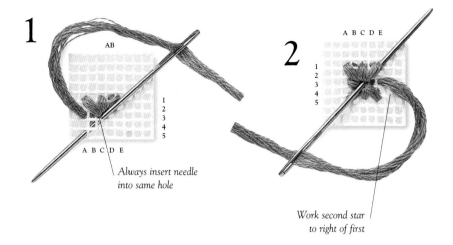

1

AB

A B C D E

1
2
3
4
5

Always insert needle into same hole

2

A B C D E

1
2
3
4
5

Work second star to right of first

····· OTHER NAME ·····
Algerian eye stitch

········· LEVEL ·········
Intermediate

·········· USES ··········
Fine textured filling

········ METHOD ········
Straight stitch stars worked in horizontal rows

······ MATERIALS ······
Single canvas; thick thread

1 Start at top left with four straight stitches from **1E** to **3C**, **1C** to **3C**, **1A** to **3C** and **3A** to **3C**.

2 Work four more stitches to complete the star, from **5A** to **3C**, **5C** to **3C**, **5E** to **3C** and **3E** to **3C**. Begin the next star at **1E** and repeat steps 1 and 2 to continue. Work the next row directly below.

Eye

1

1
2
3
4

A B C D

Enlarge center hole to accommodate 24 stitches

2

1
2
3
4
5
6
7

A B C E F

Work each stitch over three threads

Stitch in clockwise direction

········· LEVEL ·········
Intermediate

·········· USES ··········
Large scale filling

········ METHOD ········
Square blocks of straight stitch with open centers, outlined with back stitch

······ MATERIALS ······
Single canvas; thick thread; embroidery scissors

1 Start at top left. Enlarge the hole at **4D** by carefully twisting the scissor point between the canvas threads. Work two straight stitches from **1A** to **4D** and **1B** to **4D**.

2 Make eleven more stitches into **4D**, starting from **1C, 1D, 1E, 1F, 1G, 2G, 3G, 4G, 5G, 6G** and **7G**. Work the second half as a mirror image of the first, then start the next block at **1G**. Finish off by outlining each square with back stitch (see p.40), worked over one thread.

········· TECHNIQUE VARIATION ·········

The back stitch outline can be worked in a contrasting color to create a square grid pattern across the canvas.

Diamond Eye

Work each stitch over three threads

Always insert needle into same hole

·········· LEVEL ··········
Advanced

·········· USES ···········
Geometric background or filling for large areas

········· METHOD ·········
Straight stitch diamonds with open centers, outlined in back stitch

······· MATERIALS ·······
Single canvas; thick thread

1 Start at top left with an upright stitch from **1E** to **5E**. Make seven more stitches into the same hole from **2F**, **3G**, **4H**, **5I**, **6H**, **7G**, **8F** and **9E**, then work the second half of the diamond as a mirror image of the first.

2 Work the next block in the same way, starting with **5I** to **9I**, and stitch the next row directly below the first. When the area is complete, outline each diamond with back stitch (see p.40) worked over one thread to conceal any canvas that may show through.

Fan

····· OTHER NAME ·····
Ray stitch

·········· LEVEL ··········
Easy

·········· USES ···········
Fine textured filling

········· METHOD ·········
Square blocks of radiating stitches, worked in horizontal rows

······· MATERIALS ·······
Single canvas; thick thread

Insert the needle at same point for every stitch

Work stitches in opposite direction to first row

1 Starting at bottom left, make an upright stitch from **4A** to **7A**. Work six more stitches into the same hole, from **4B**, **4C**, **4D**, **5D**, **6D** and **7D**, to form a square. Start the next block at **4D** to **7D** and continue working toward the right.

2 Work the next row directly above the first and stitch in the opposite direction, starting at **1G** to **4G**. Repeat steps 1 and 2 to continue.

Looped and Tied Needlepoint Stitches

THIS GROUP INCLUDES some of the most advanced and interesting stitches, which can be used when unusual textures and multi-colored patterns are required. The looped Rya and Turkey stitches, traditionally used for rugs, are ideal for stitching raised areas within a design and can be trimmed to give a plush finish. The tied and twisted stitches consist of long straight stitches held down with shorter stitches to give a dense, ridged surface. All the stitches in this section should be worked in a frame on single canvas. Make sure that the thread or yarn used covers all of the background threads.

Rya

Looped thread forms diagonal stitch

2

Hold loose end down when pulling needle through

3

A B C D

·········· **LEVEL** ··········
Advanced

········· **USES** ·········
Looped or cut pile stitch for carpet-like texture

········· **METHOD** ·········
Looped stitch worked over knitting needle in horizontal rows

········· **MATERIALS** ·········
Single canvas; thick thread; knitting needle

1 Start at bottom left. Take the needle down at **1A** and bring it through at **2A**, leaving a short tail. Insert at **1B** and come back out at **1A**.

2 Pass the needle back under the diagonal loop and pull both ends tightly. Hold the knitting needle below the stitches and take the thread over and under it to form a loop.

3 Repeat steps 1 and 2 to continue, starting the second stitch at **1B**. Work the next and subsquent rows directly above the first. Trim the pile if a tufted effect is desired.

Turkey

Pull needle through below working thread

1

A B C

2 A B C D

3

Keep loops same length

A B C D E F G H I J

Hold loop down while making next stitch

········· **OTHER NAME** ·········
Ghiordes knot stitch

········· **LEVEL** ·········
Advanced

········· **USES** ·········
Tufted filling; background

········· **METHOD** ·········
Looped stitch, with cut pile

········· **MATERIALS** ·········
Single or rug canvas; thick thread or yarn

1 Start at bottom left. Insert the needle at **1B** and bring it out at **1A**. Take it down at **1C** and come out again at **1B**.

2 Repeat step 1, starting at **1D**. Leave a loop of thread between the stitches.

3 Continue working toward the right, making sure the loops are the same length. Work each following row one space above. When the stitching is complete, cut and trim the loops to create a pile.

Houndstooth

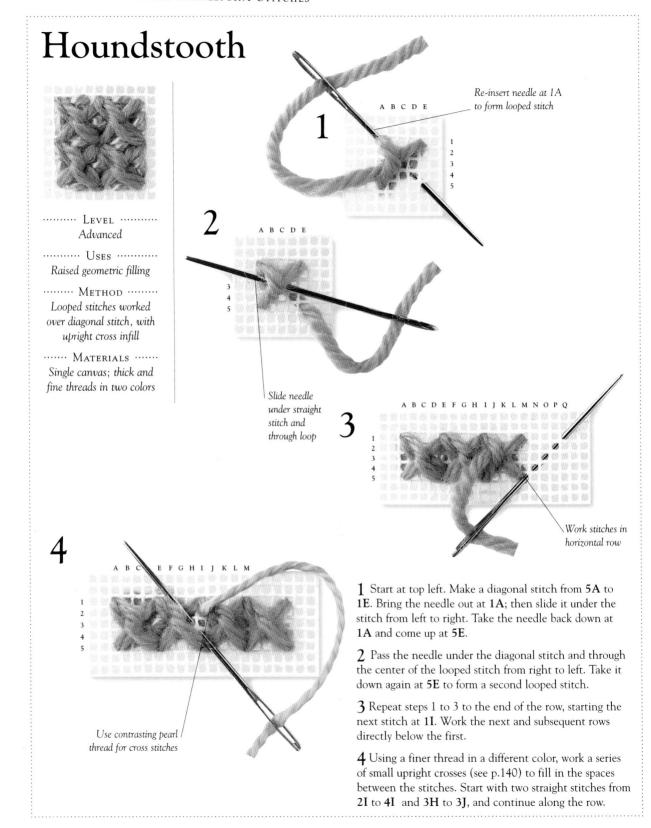

Re-insert needle at 1A to form looped stitch

LEVEL
Advanced

USES
Raised geometric filling

METHOD
Looped stitches worked over diagonal stitch, with upright cross infill

MATERIALS
Single canvas; thick and fine threads in two colors

Slide needle under straight stitch and through loop

Work stitches in horizontal row

Use contrasting pearl thread for cross stitches

1 Start at top left. Make a diagonal stitch from **5A** to **1E**. Bring the needle out at **1A**; then slide it under the stitch from left to right. Take the needle back down at **1A** and come up at **5E**.

2 Pass the needle under the diagonal stitch and through the center of the looped stitch from right to left. Take it down again at **5E** to form a second looped stitch.

3 Repeat steps 1 to 3 to the end of the row, starting the next stitch at **1I**. Work the next and subsequent rows directly below the first.

4 Using a finer thread in a different color, work a series of small upright crosses (see p.140) to fill in the spaces between the stitches. Start with two straight stitches from **2I** to **4I** and **3H** to **3J**, and continue along the row.

Knitting

·········· LEVEL ··········
Easy

·········· USES ··········
Filling resembling knitted stocking stitch

·········· METHOD ··········
Overlapping diagonal stitches worked vertically in alternate directions

·········· MATERIALS ··········
Single canvas; any thread

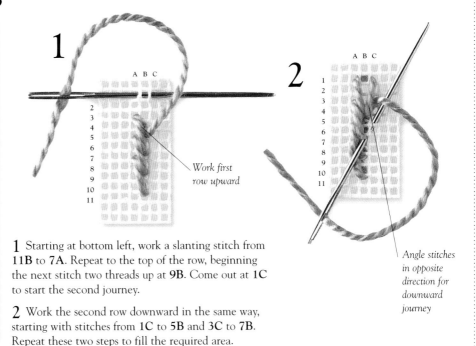

1

A B C

Work first row upward

2

A B C

Angle stitches in opposite direction for downward journey

1 Starting at bottom left, work a slanting stitch from **11B** to **7A**. Repeat to the top of the row, beginning the next stitch two threads up at **9B**. Come out at **1C** to start the second journey.

2 Work the second row downward in the same way, starting with stitches from **1C** to **5B** and **3C** to **7B**. Repeat these two steps to fill the required area.

Old Wheatsheaf

·········· LEVEL ··········
Advanced

·········· USES ··········
In single row as border; filling for large areas

·········· METHOD ··········
Sheaf stitch variation with contrast interlacing

·········· MATERIALS ··········
Single canvas; any thread in two contrasting colors

1

Pull thread tightly to bunch upright stitches together

A B C D

2

A B   D E F G H   J

Work interlacing in contrasting colour

1 Start at top left. Work four upright stitches from **7A** to **1A**, **7B** to **1B**, **7C** to **1C**, and **7D** to **1D**. Bring the needle up behind the stitches at **4B** and insert it at **4C** to make a tie stitch (see p.20). Start the next sheaf at **7D** to **1D**. Work the following rows directly below the first.

2 Using the second thread, bring the needle up at **3A**. Slide it downward below the tie stitch, and insert at **5A**. Come up at **3D**, pass the needle under the tie stitch again, and take it down at **5D**. Lace each sheaf in the same way.

Tied Gobelin

····· OTHER NAME ·····
Knotted stitch

········· LEVEL ·········
Intermediate

··········· USES ···········
Filling with ridged texture

········· METHOD ·········
*Horizontal rows of
interlocking tied diagonal
stitches*

······· MATERIALS ·······
Single canvas; any thread

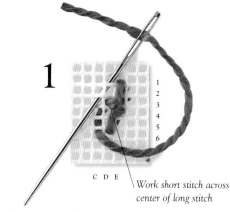

*Work short stitch across
center of long stitch*

1 Start at top right. Work a long diagonal stitch
from **6D** to **1E**, crossed by a short stitch from **4E** to
3D. Make the next pair of stitches from **6C** to **1D**
and **3C** to **4D**, and continue working to the left.

2 The next row is stitched in the opposite direction.
Work the first two stitches from **9A** to **4B** and **7B** to
6A and repeat to the end of the row.. Repeat these
two rows to fill the required area.

*Insert needle into
hole at base of
tie stitch*

French

········· LEVEL ·········
Intermediate

··········· USES ···········
*Textured, ridged filling
or background*

········· METHOD ·········
*Pairs of tied upright
stitches worked in
horizontal rows*

······· MATERIALS ·······
Single canvas; any thread

*Work both upright
stitches in same holes*

1 Start at top left. Make an upright stitch from **7B** to
1B held down by a tie stitch (see p.20) from **4B** to **4A**.
Work a second upright stitch from **7B** to **1B** and anchor
it with a tie stitch from **4C** to **4B**. Continue making
pairs of tied stitches to the end of the row.

2 Work the next row in the opposite direction, starting
with an upright stitch from **10E** to **4E** and a tie stitch
from **7E** to **7F**. Repeat these two rows to continue.

*Work second row
into spaces between
first pairs of stitches*

Pineapple

········ LEVEL ········
Advanced

········· USES ·········
Two-colored geometric filling for large areas

········ METHOD ········
Tied cross stitches worked over upright Gobelin stitch

······ MATERIALS ·······
Single canvas; any thread in two colors

Work upright stitches in a multiple of five

Work tie stitch over cross

Insert needle between upright stitches

1 Start at top left and work a row of upright Gobelin stitch (see p.119) starting at **5A** to **1A**. Using the second thread, make a diagonal stitch from **5A** to **1E** and come out at **5E**.

2 Insert the needle at **1A** to complete the cross, then make a horizontal tie stitch (see p.20) from **3B** to **3D**. Continue working crosses along the row, then work subsequent rows directly below.

Arrow

········ LEVEL ········
Intermediate

········· USES ·········
Textured filling; in single rows as a border

········ METHOD ········
Angled variation of sheaf filling, worked in rows

······ MATERIALS ·······
Single canvas; any thread

Work upright stitches over four threads

Pull thread up tightly to draw stitches to right

1 Starting in the top left corner, work three upright stitches from **5A** to **1A**, **5B** to **1B**, and **5C** to **1C**. Bring the needle out at **3D** and slide it under the three stitches from right to left.

2 Take the needle back down at **3D** and bring it out at **5C**, ready to make the next upright stitch. Repeat steps 1 and 2 to continue, and work the following rows directly below the first.

Index

Acknowledgments

Author's acknowledgments

No writer can work in isolation, and this book would not have been possible without the joint skills of the art and editorial teams at both Dorling Kindersley and C&B Packaging. I would like to extend my thanks to all the many colleagues and friends who have contributed their experience and commitment over the past year.

I am indebted to Samantha Gray, who first suggested my name to the publishers. Nigel Duffield, Mary Lindsay, Sarah Hall, and Cathy Shilling at DK have given me every encouragement, along with their invaluable guidance and enthusiasm, from the outset.

Managing editor Kate Yeates has been my mainstay: her dedication and constant good humor have helped me through to the end of the project. Special thanks also to Roger Bristow and Helen Collins at C&B Packaging for their invaluable creative input, to Sam Lloyd for patiently photographing all the many stitch samples, and to Heather Dewhurst for editing my text so meticulously.

Lis Gunner embroidered my designs for the chapter openers and gave me useful advice about stitching. Debbie Kilby of *Anything Left-Handed* advised me on techniques for left-handed workers.

Finally, I must thank my husband Jonathan Hayden-Williams for always being there for me, and my sister Emma Ganderton and father Colin Ganderton for their unfailing support, for which I am ever grateful.

Dorling Kindersley would like to thank the following:

DMC Creative World Ltd for supplying the needles, pearl cottons, tapestry yarns, evenweave linen, and canvas used to create the step-by-step examples and finished stitch samples. Thanks in particular to Cara Ackerman for all her help.

Additional assistance

Editorial: Nicola Munro
Design: Cathy Shilling
Administration: Christopher Gordon
Additional Photography: (p.12)
Andy Crawford, Steve Gorton

For the US edition

Thanks to Karen Kunkel for research assistance